EASY

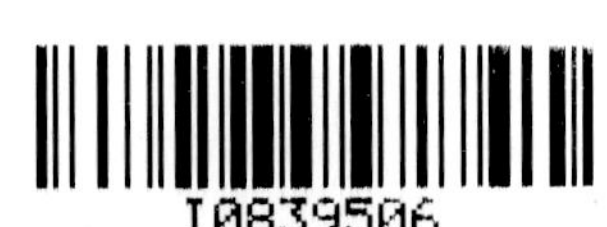

MANDALA MEDITATION COLORING BOOK

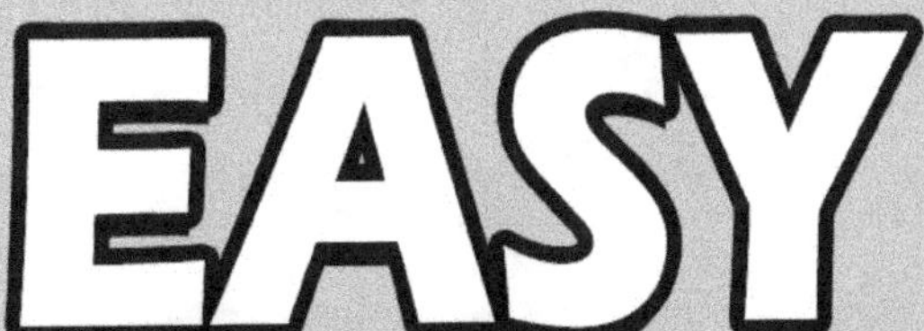

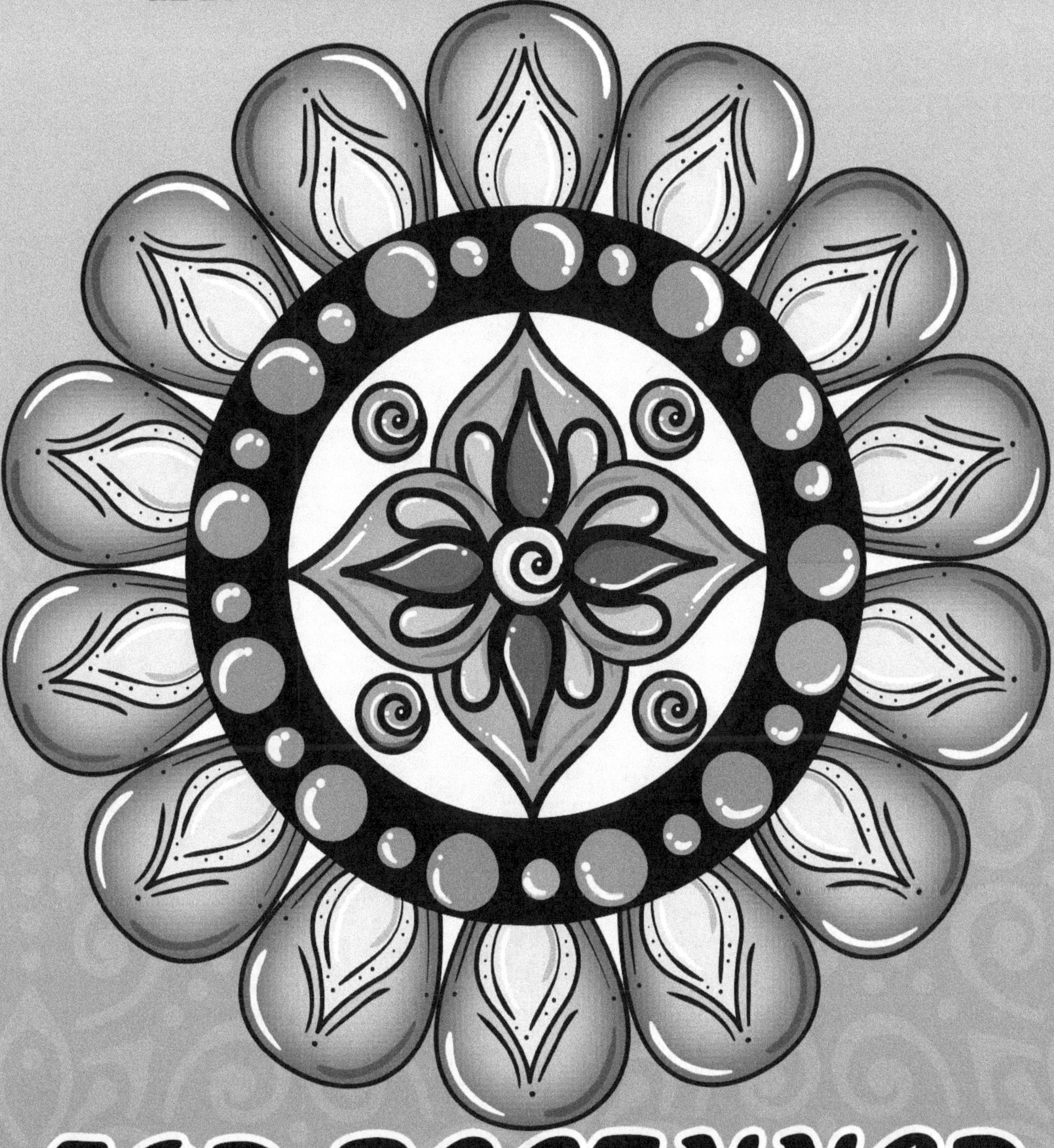

FOR BEGINNER

PUBLISHED IN 2018 BY
KODOMO PUBLISHING

PRINTED IN THE UNITED STATES OF AMERICA

COLOR TEST PAGE

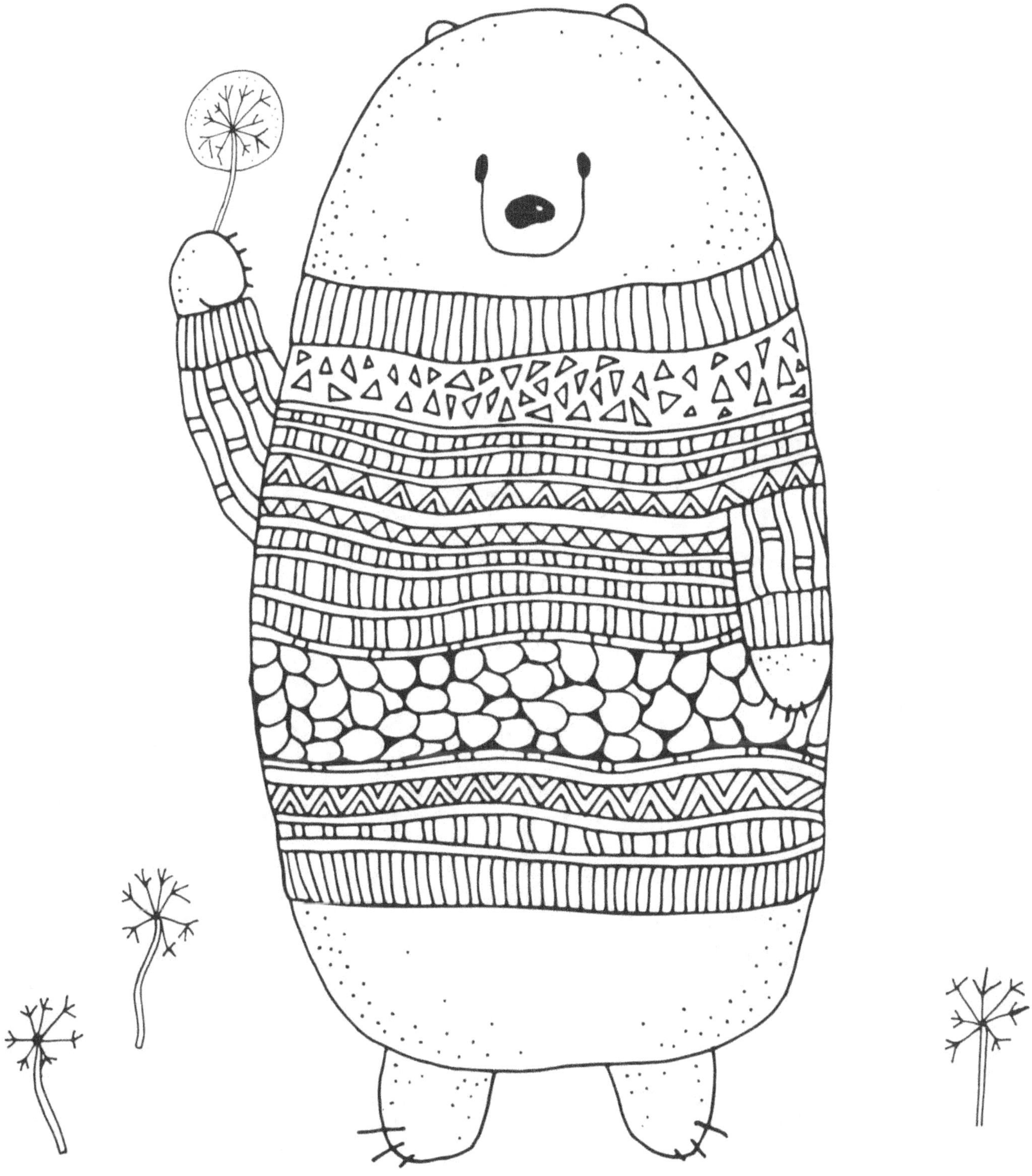

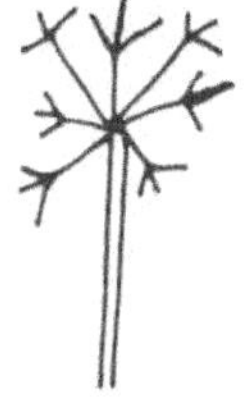

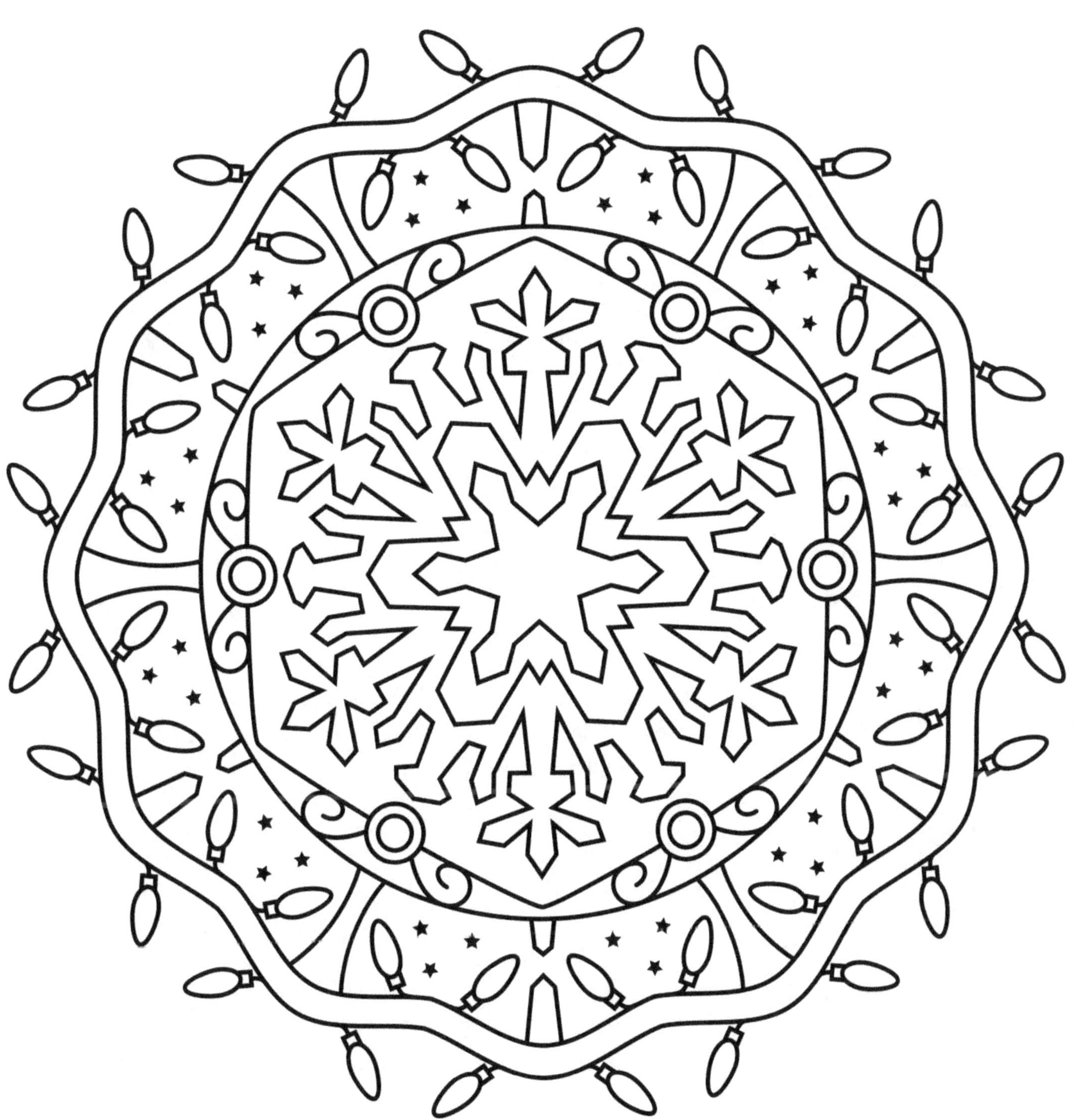

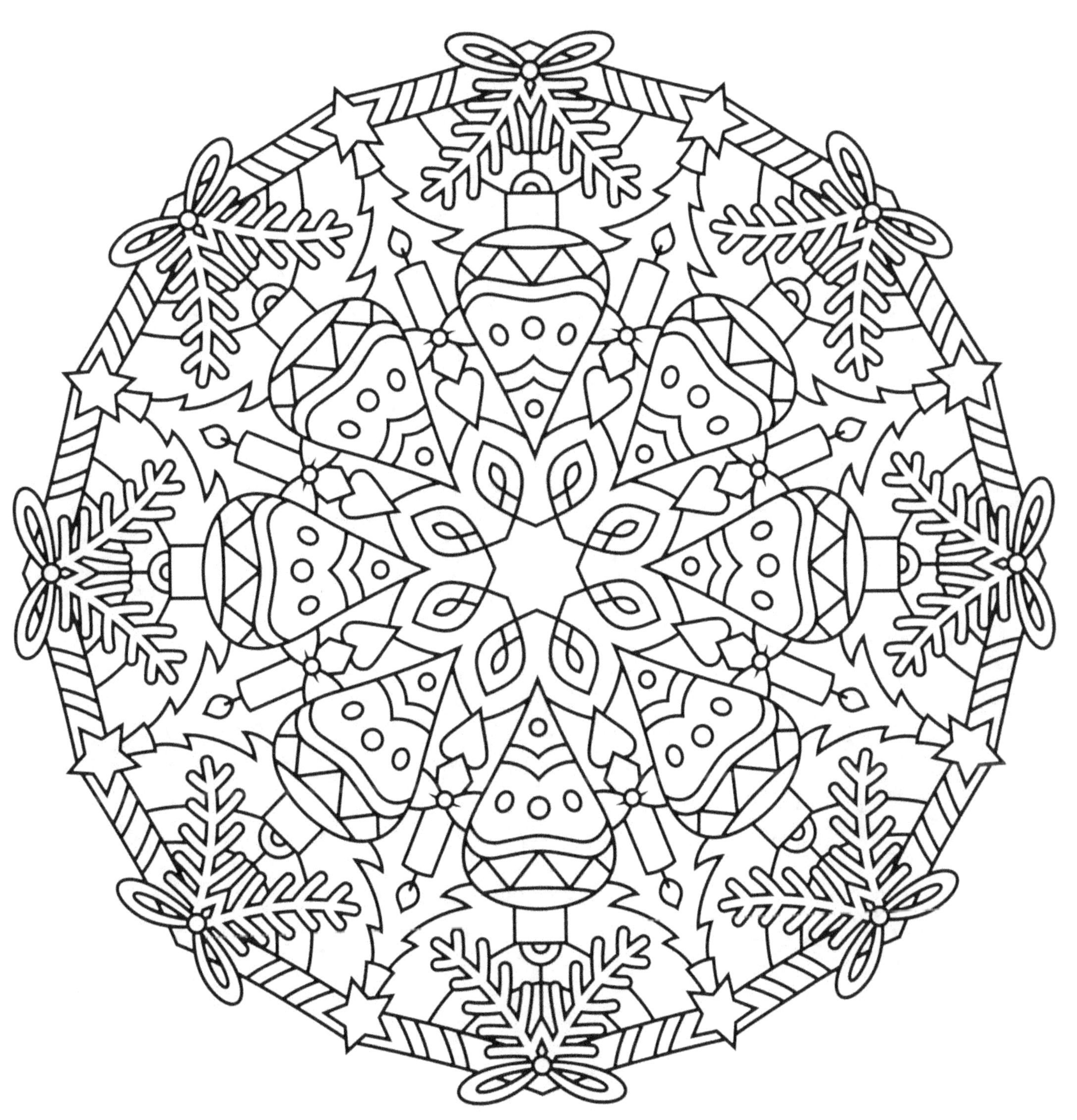

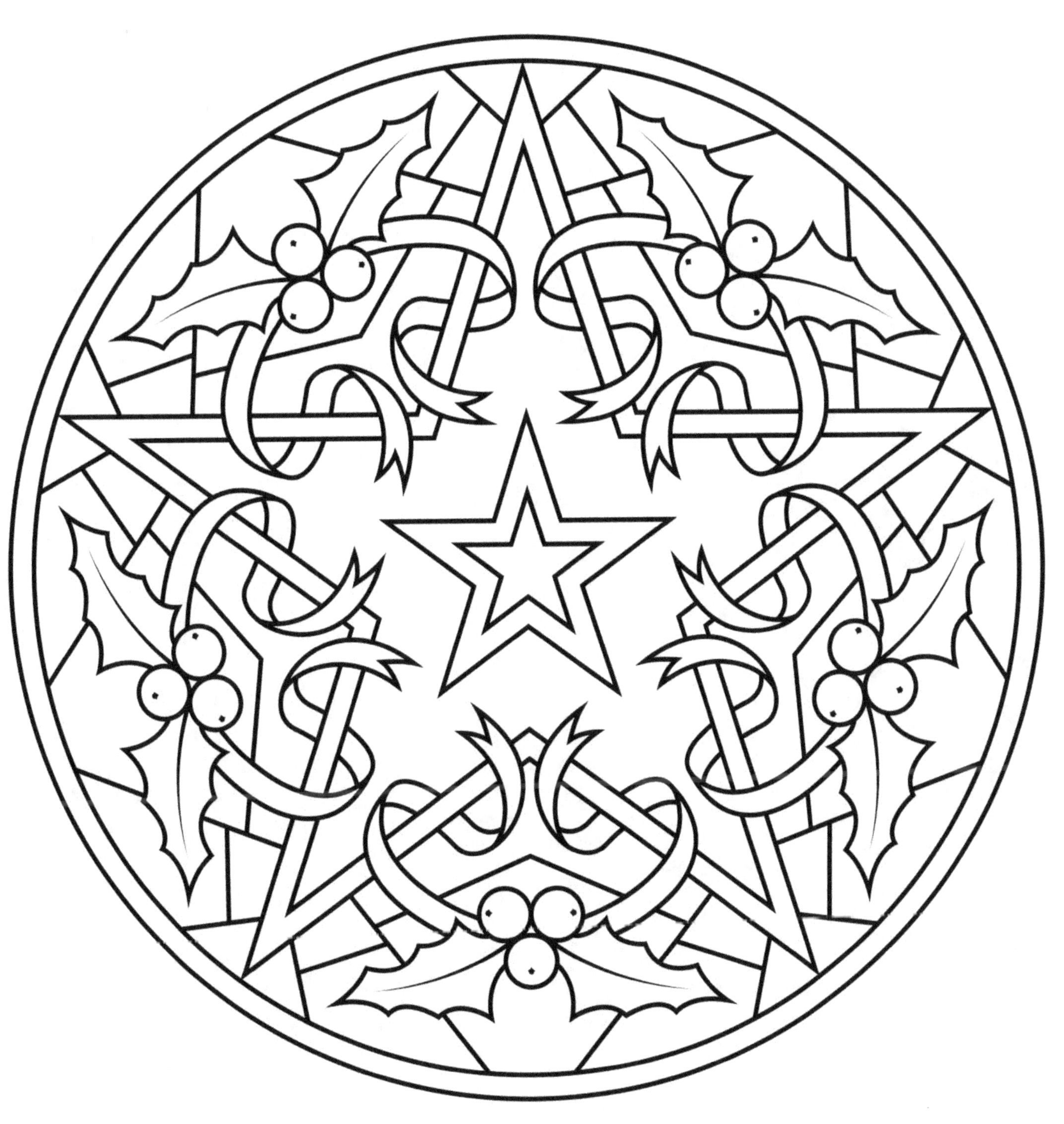

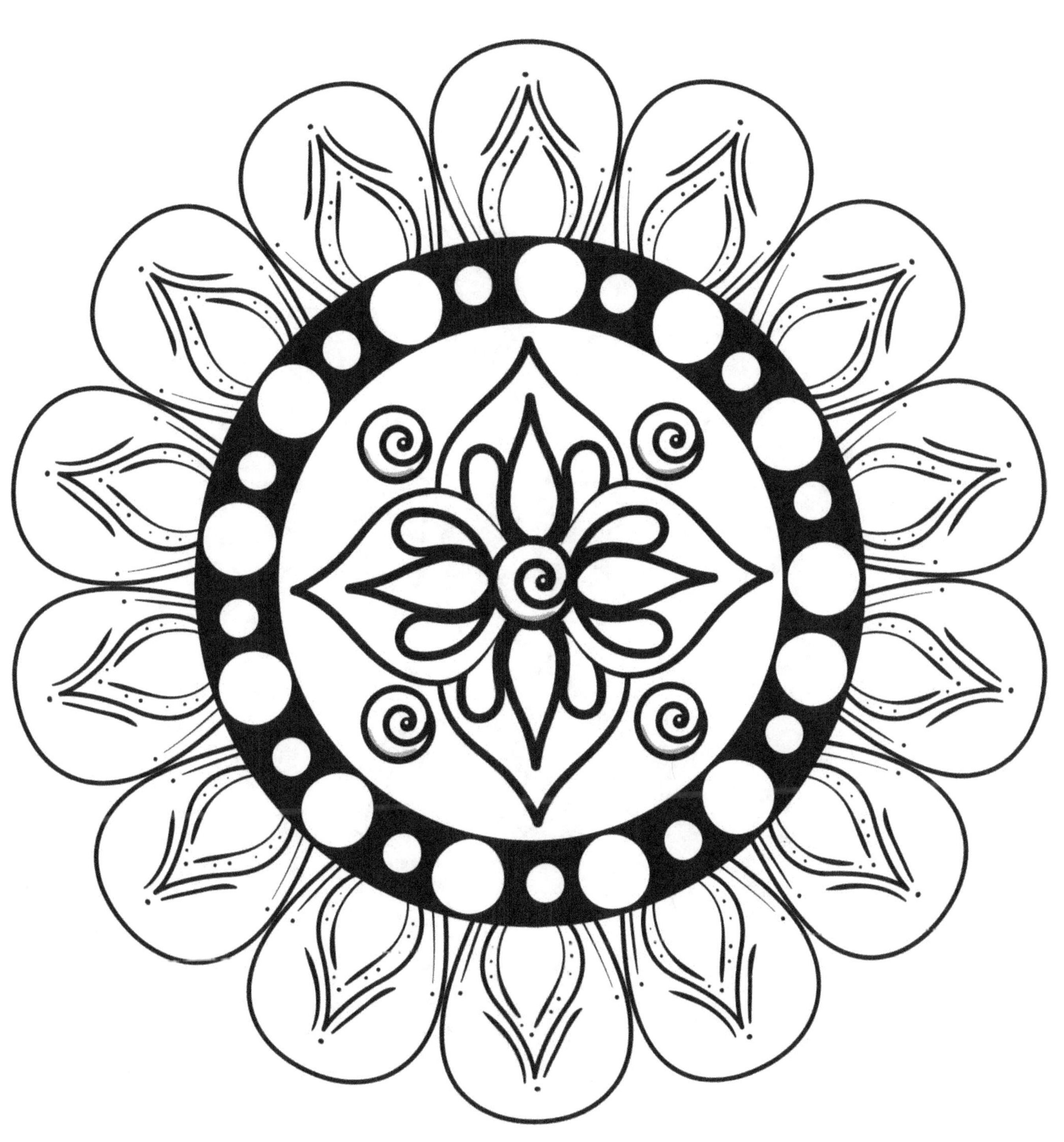

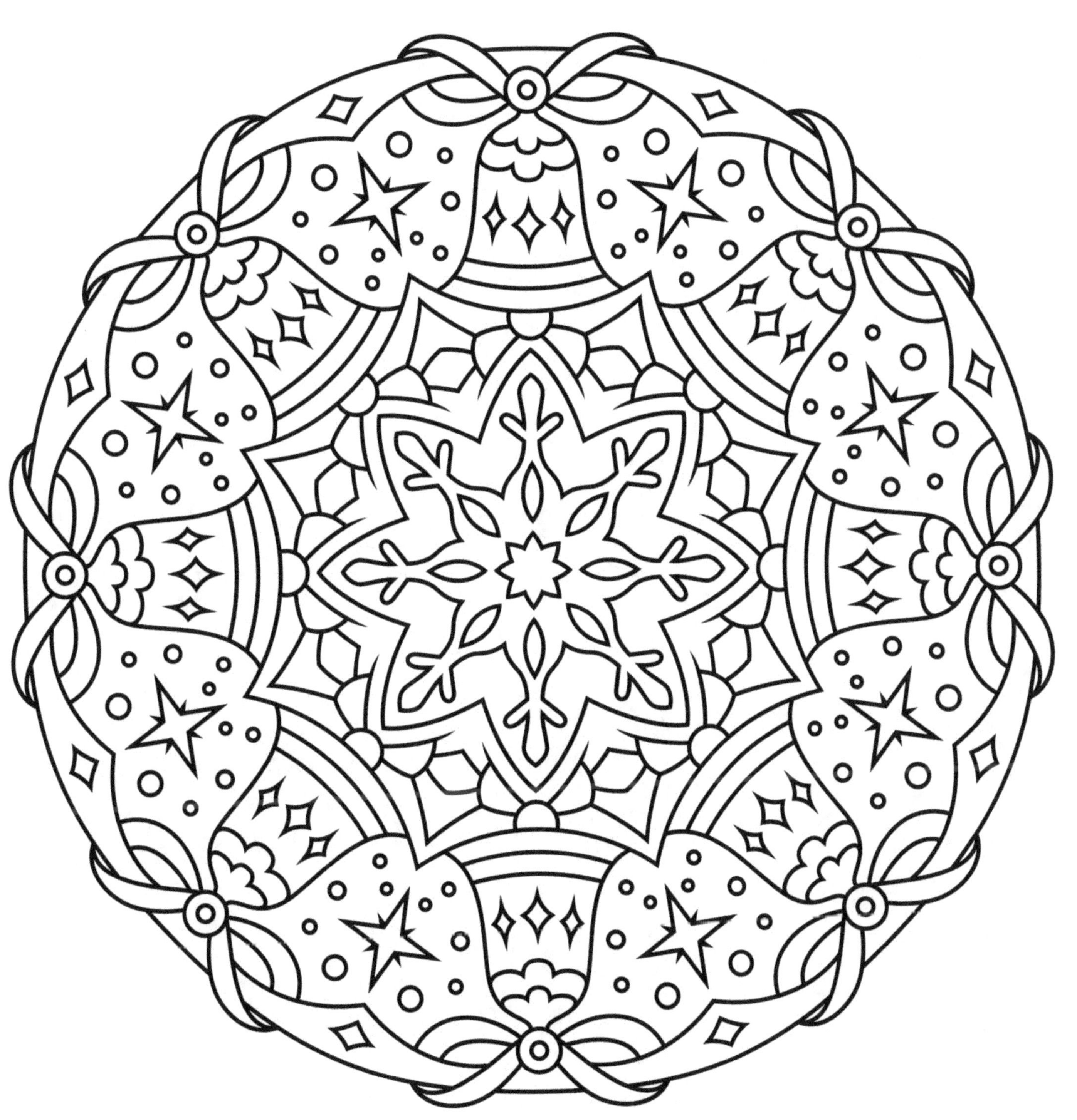

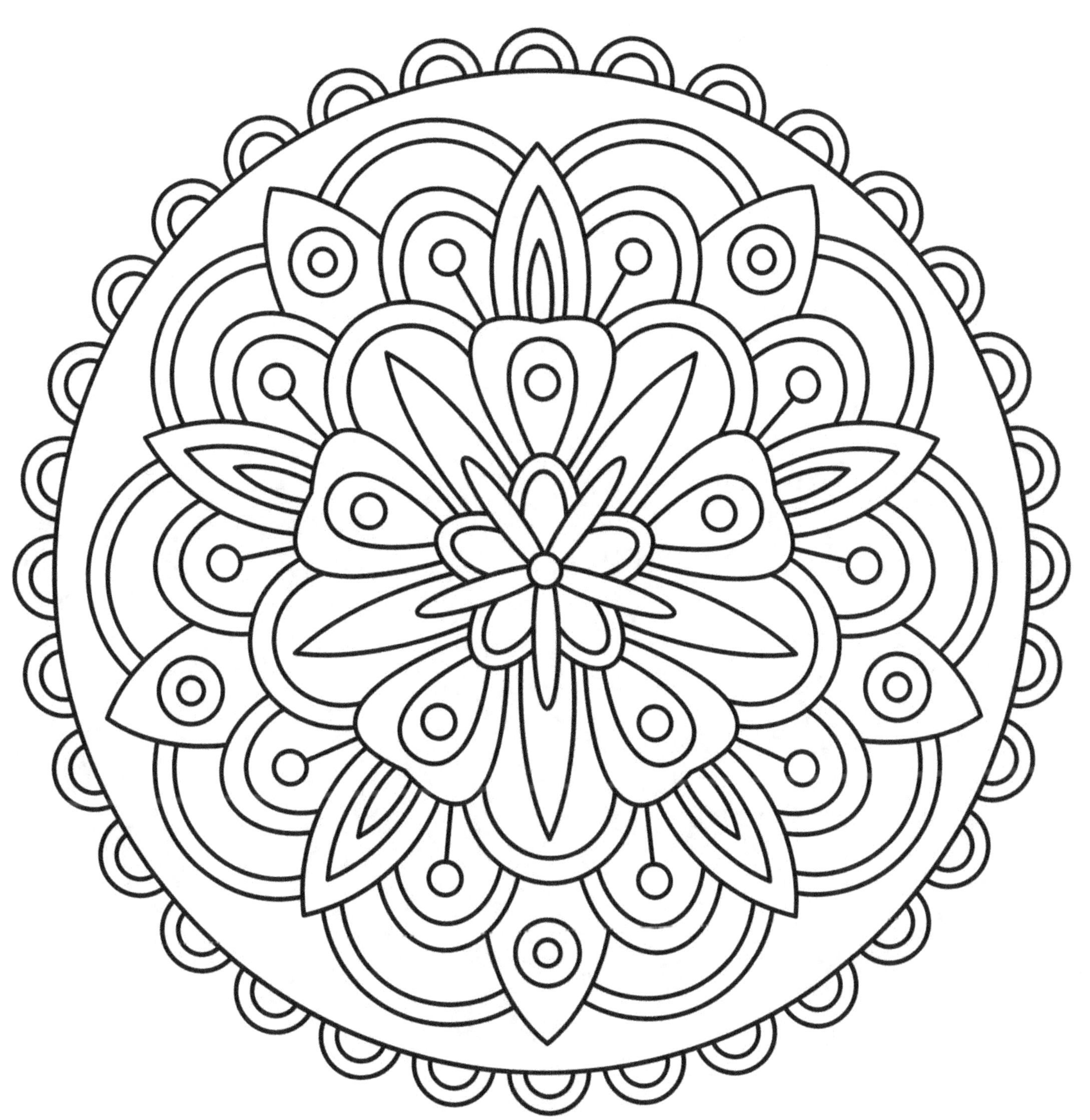

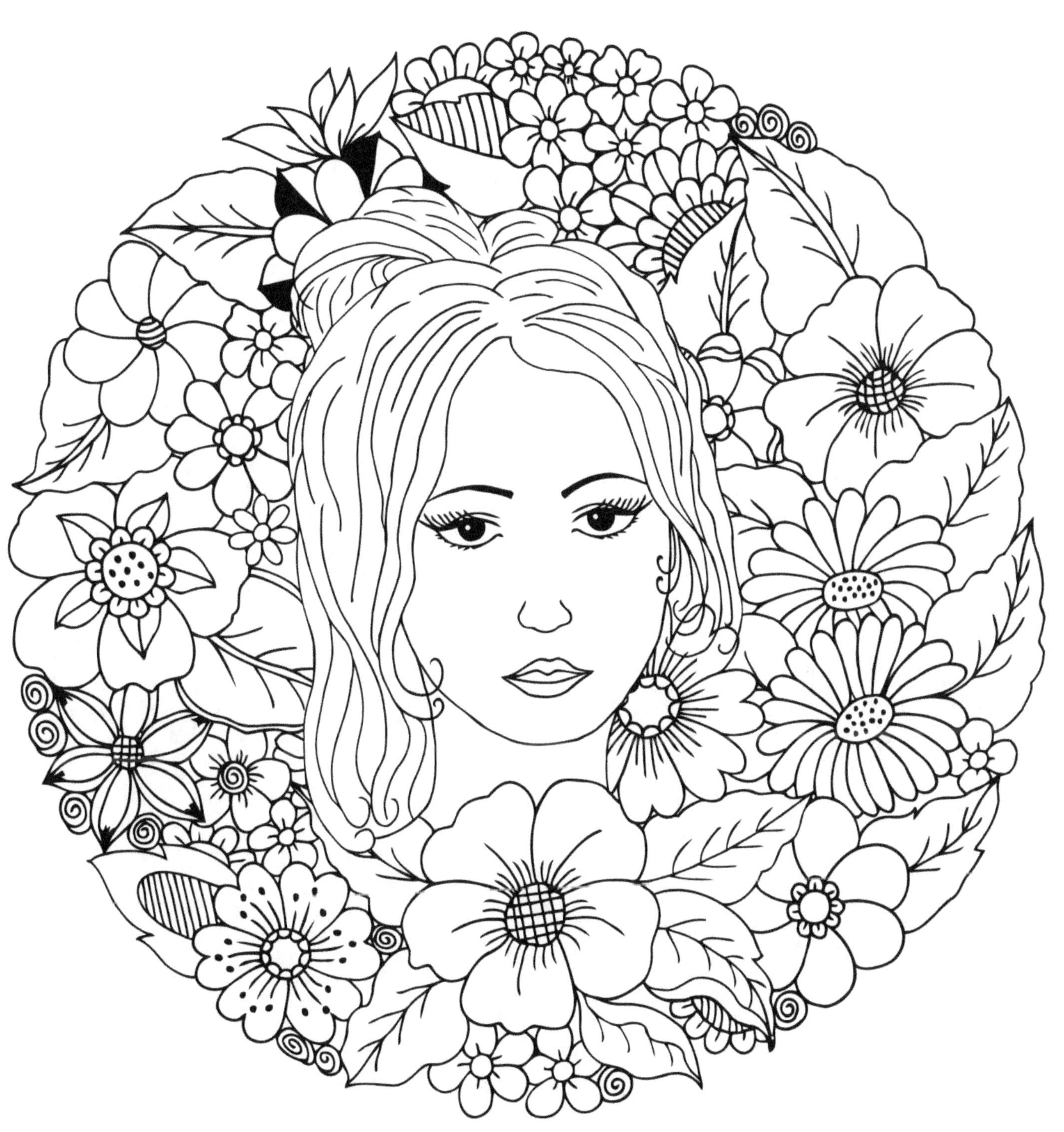

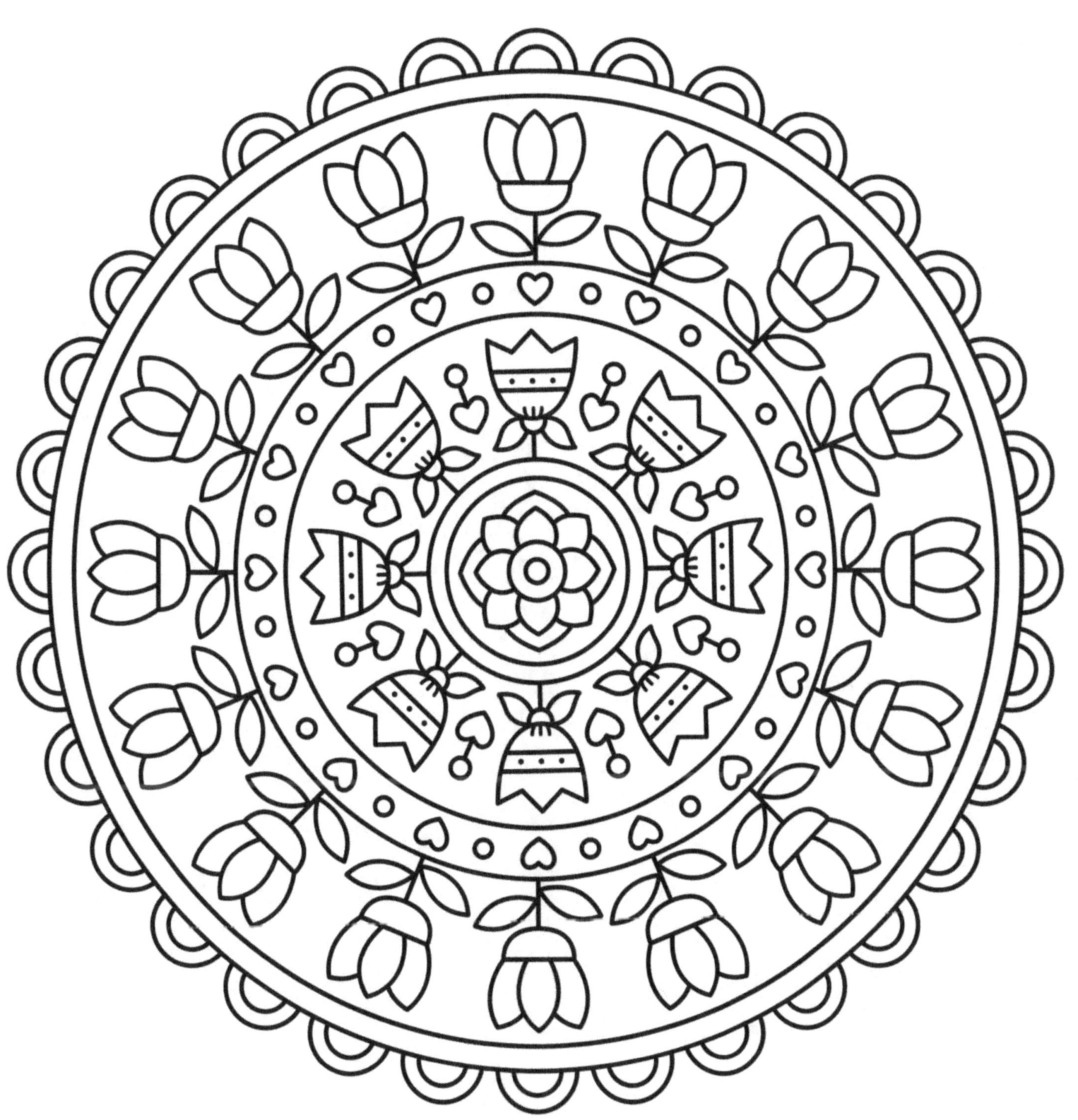

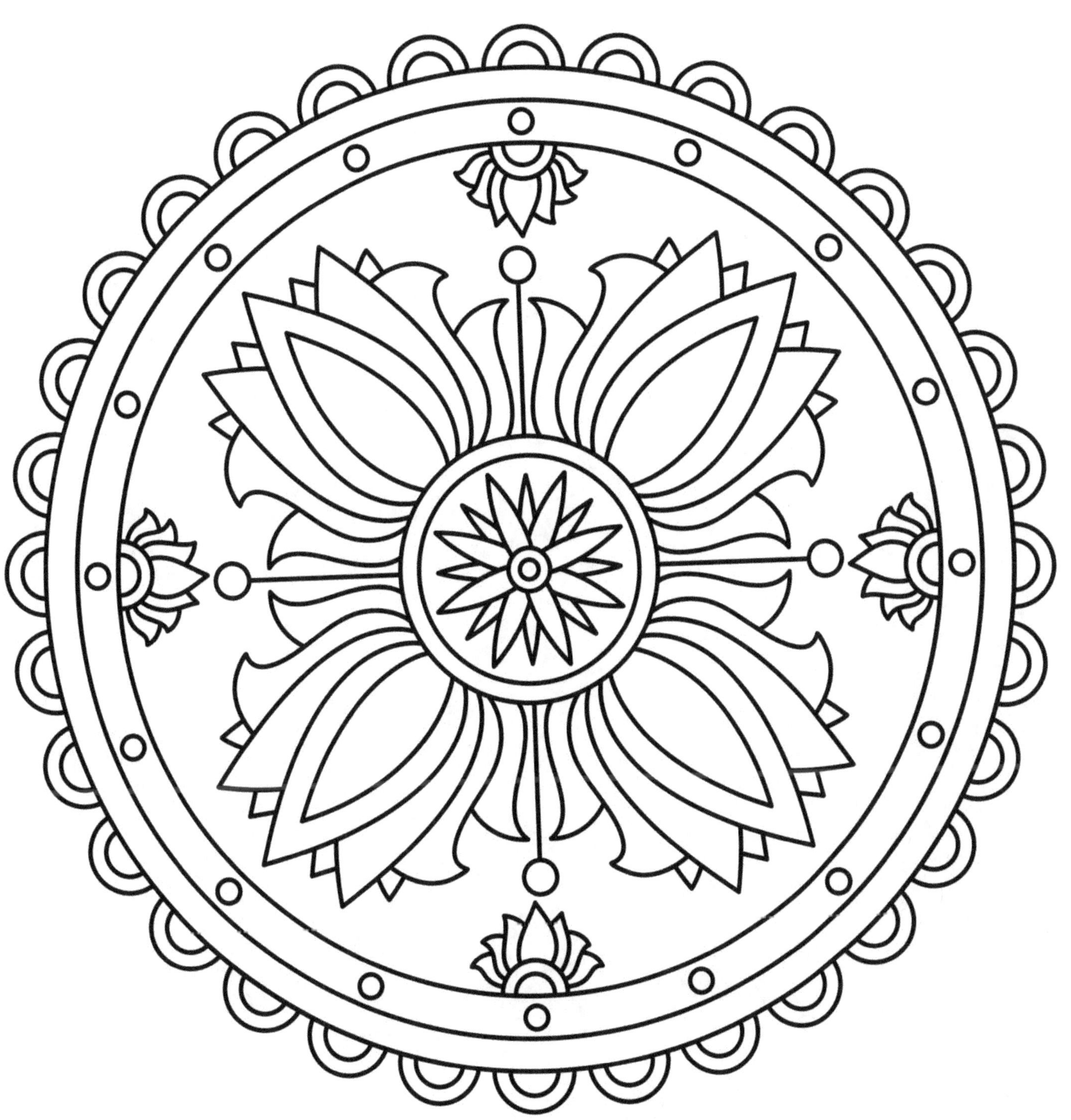

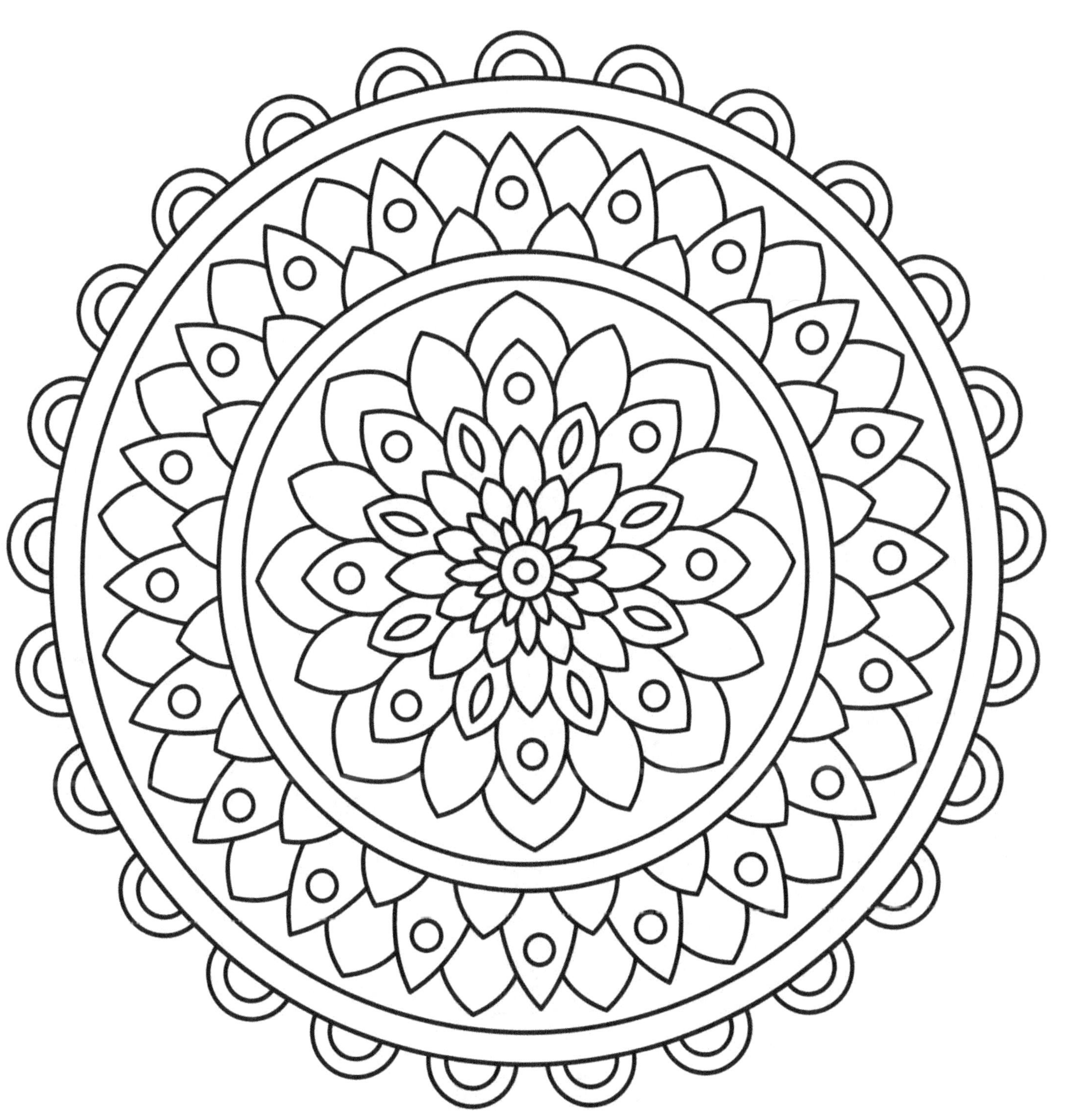

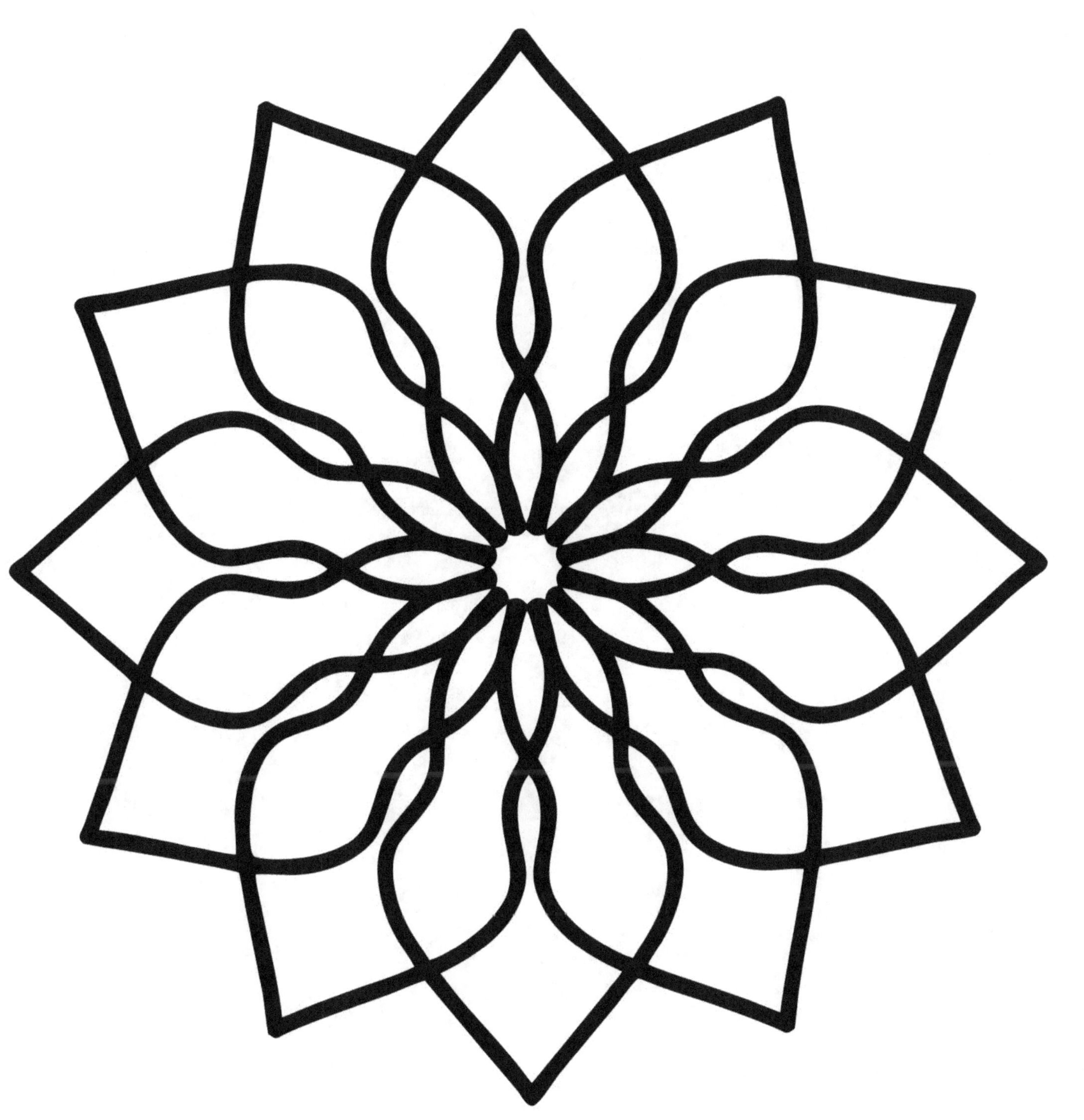

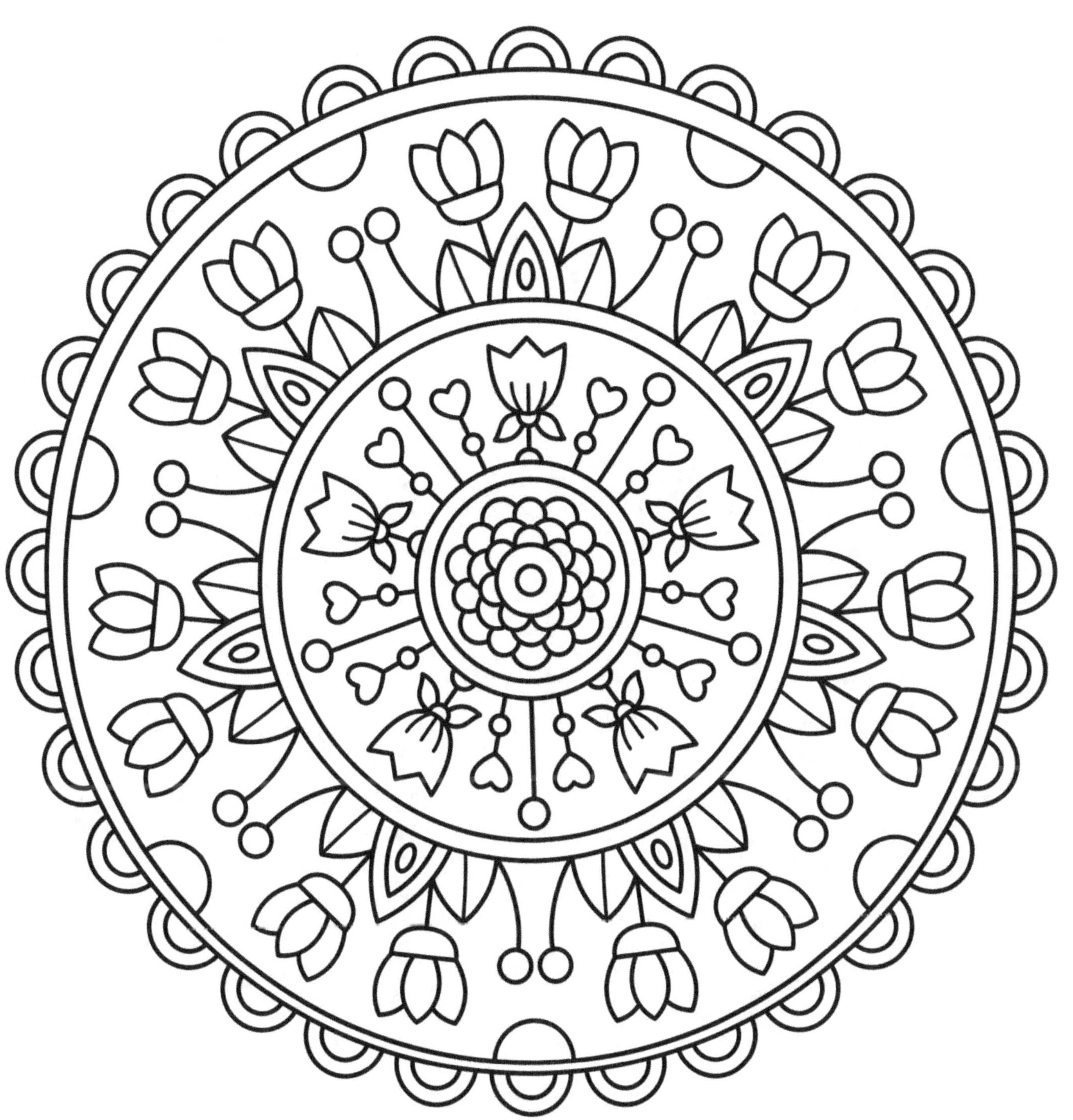

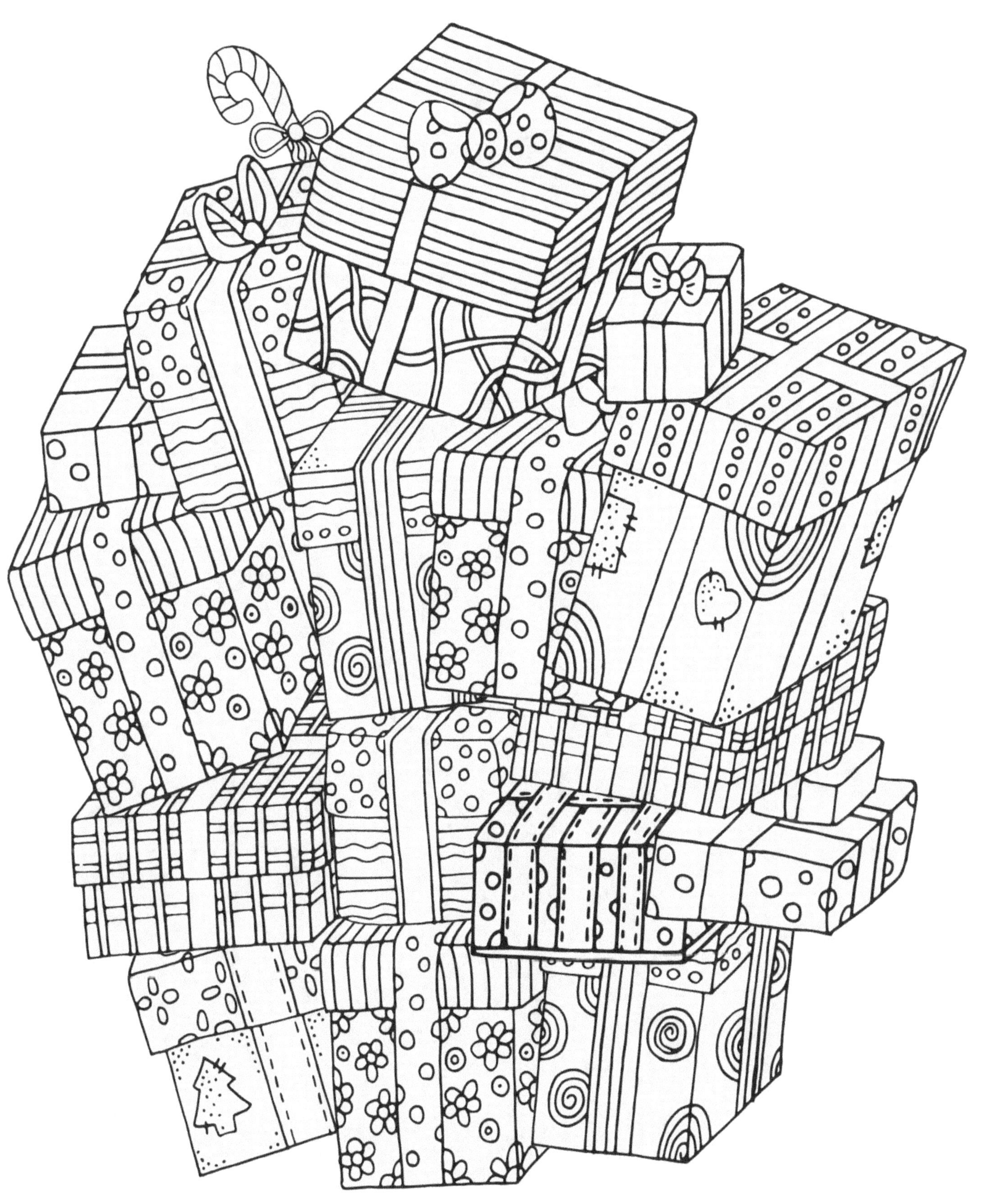

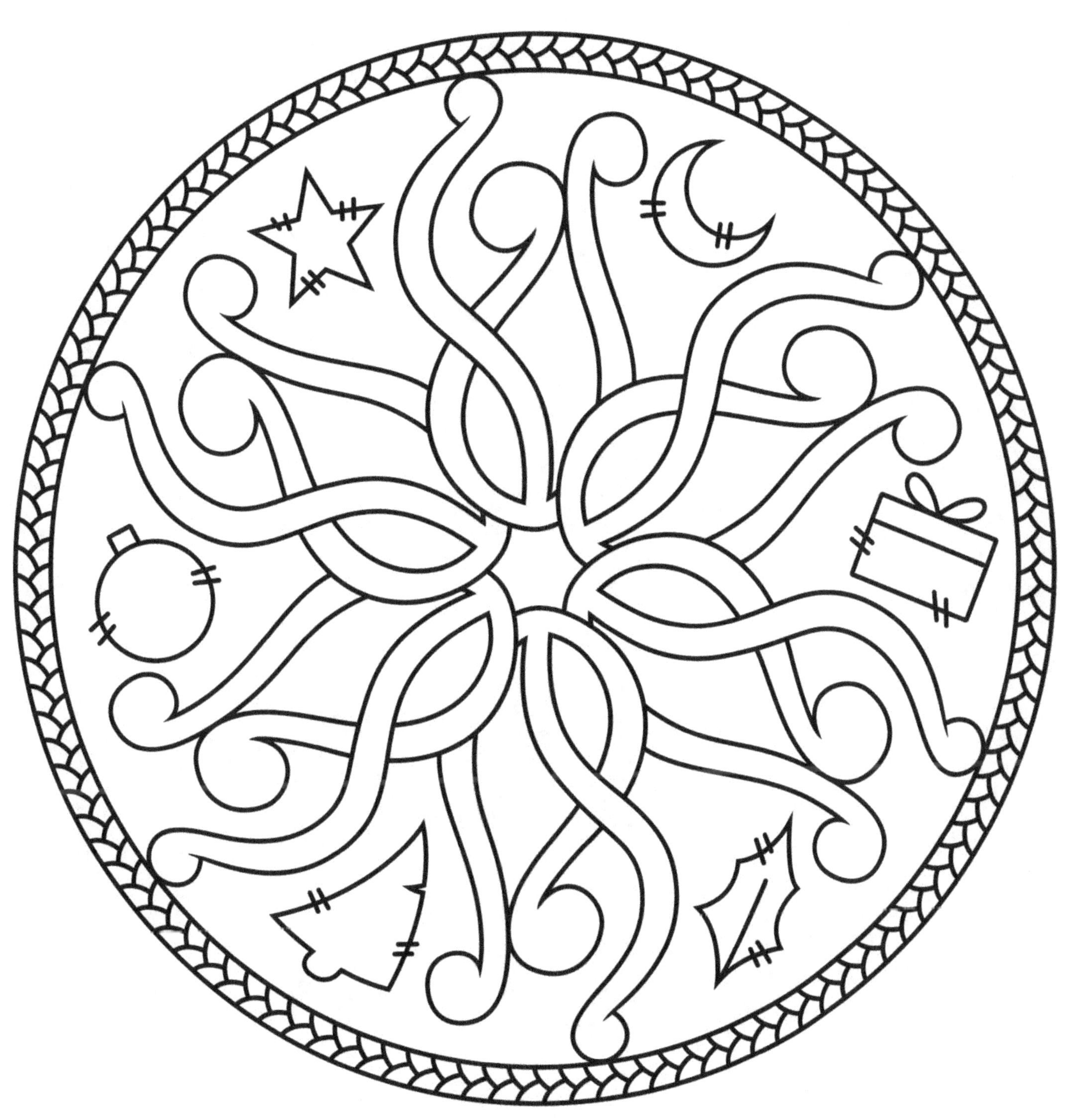

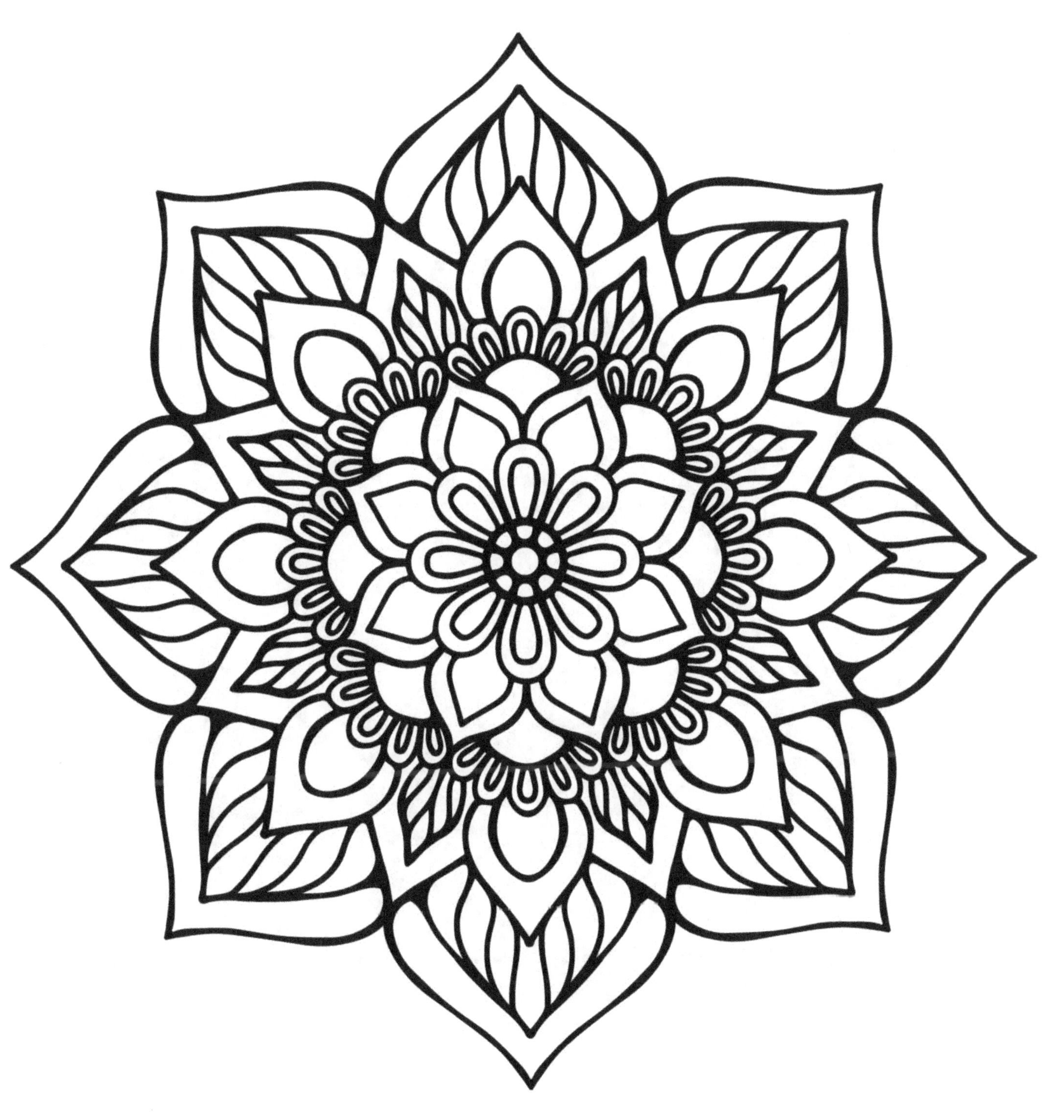

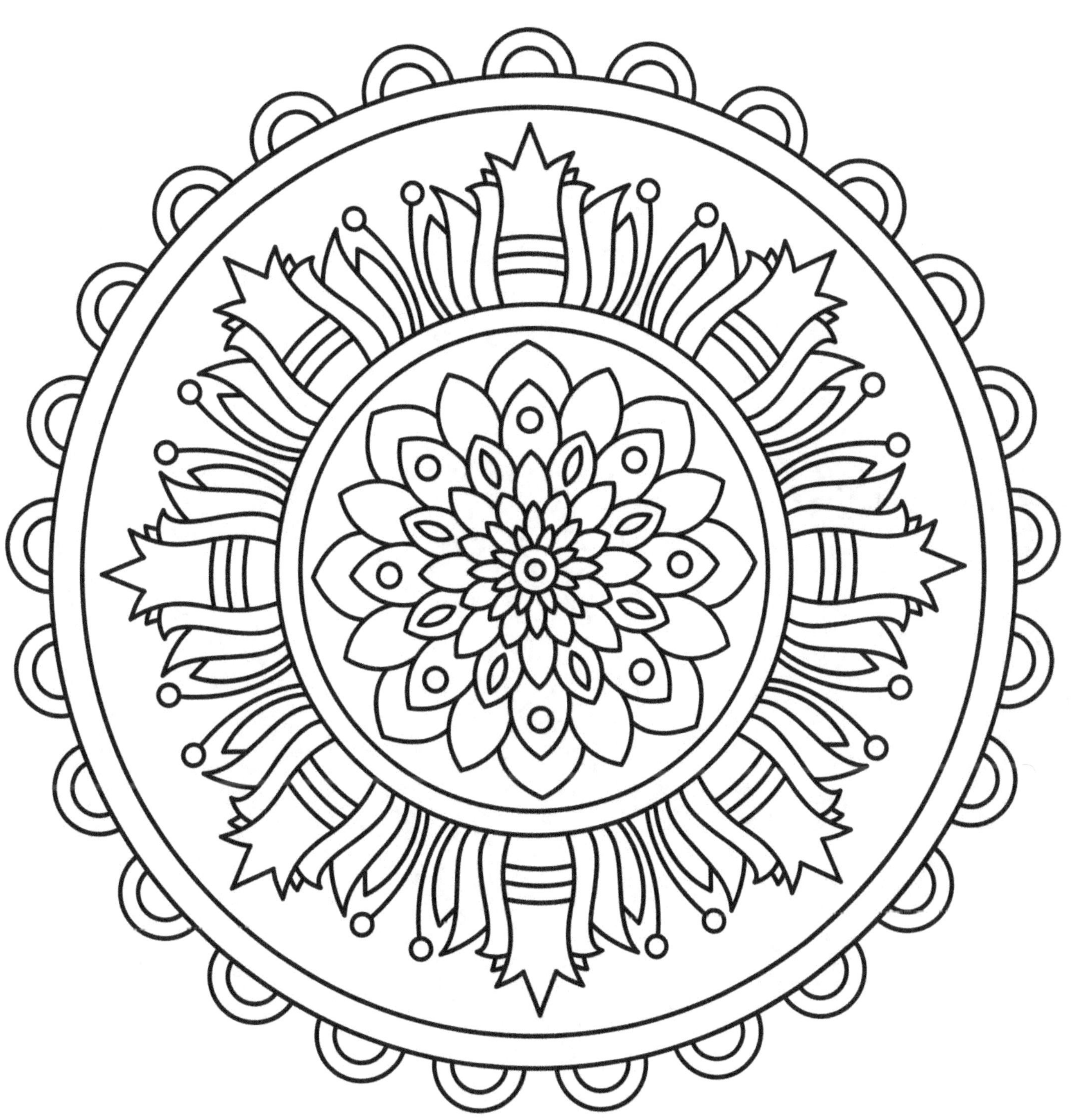

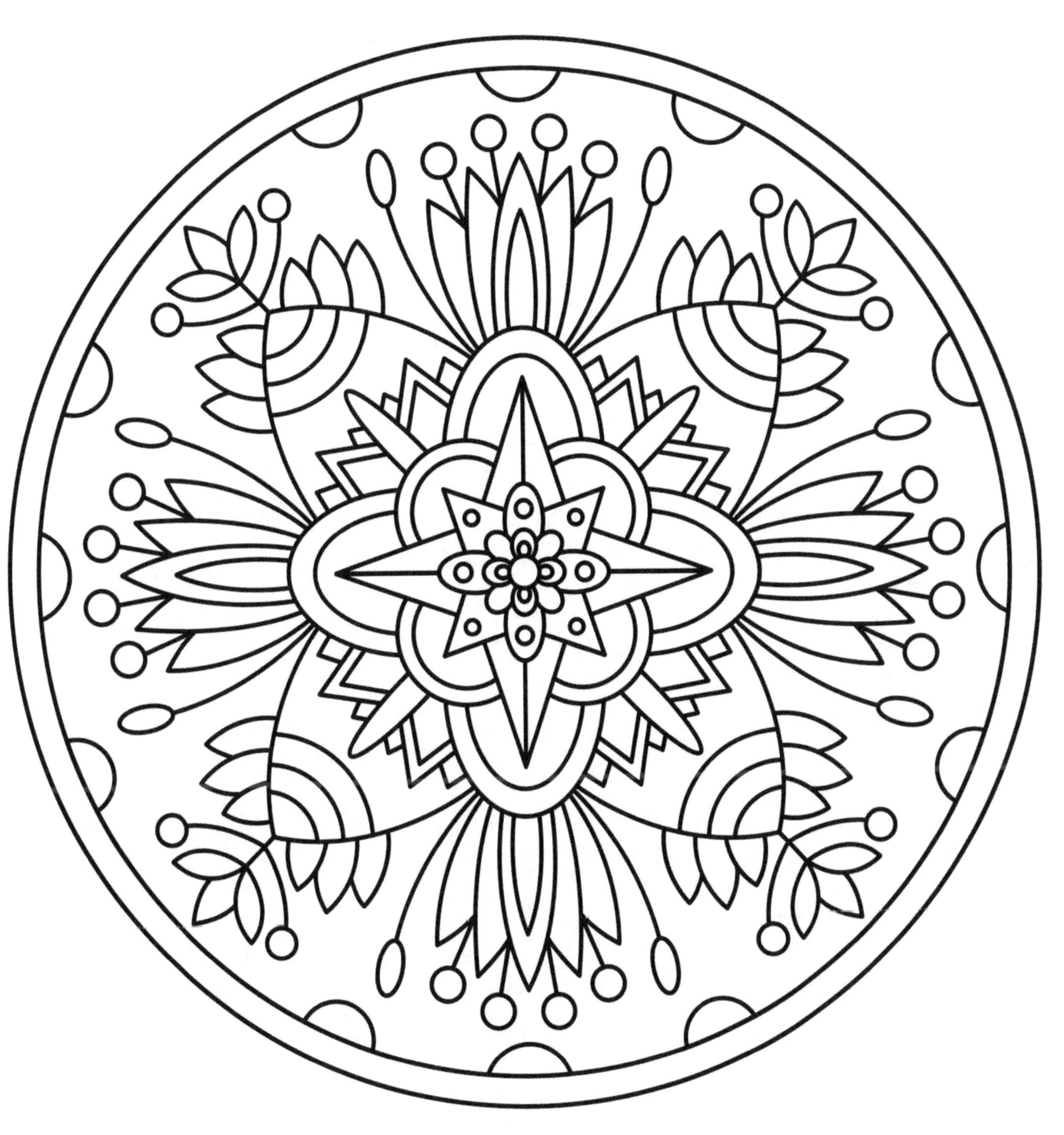

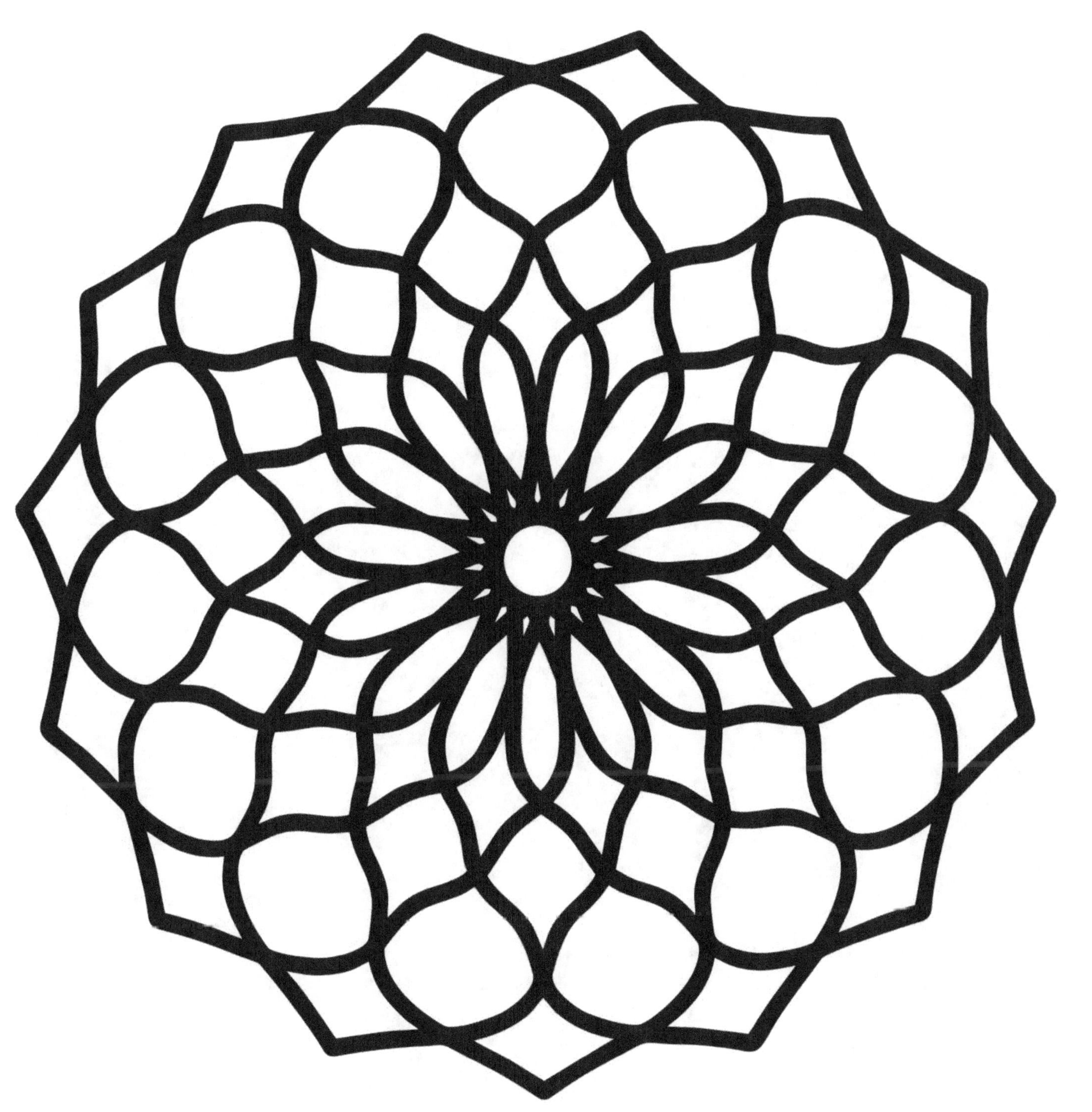

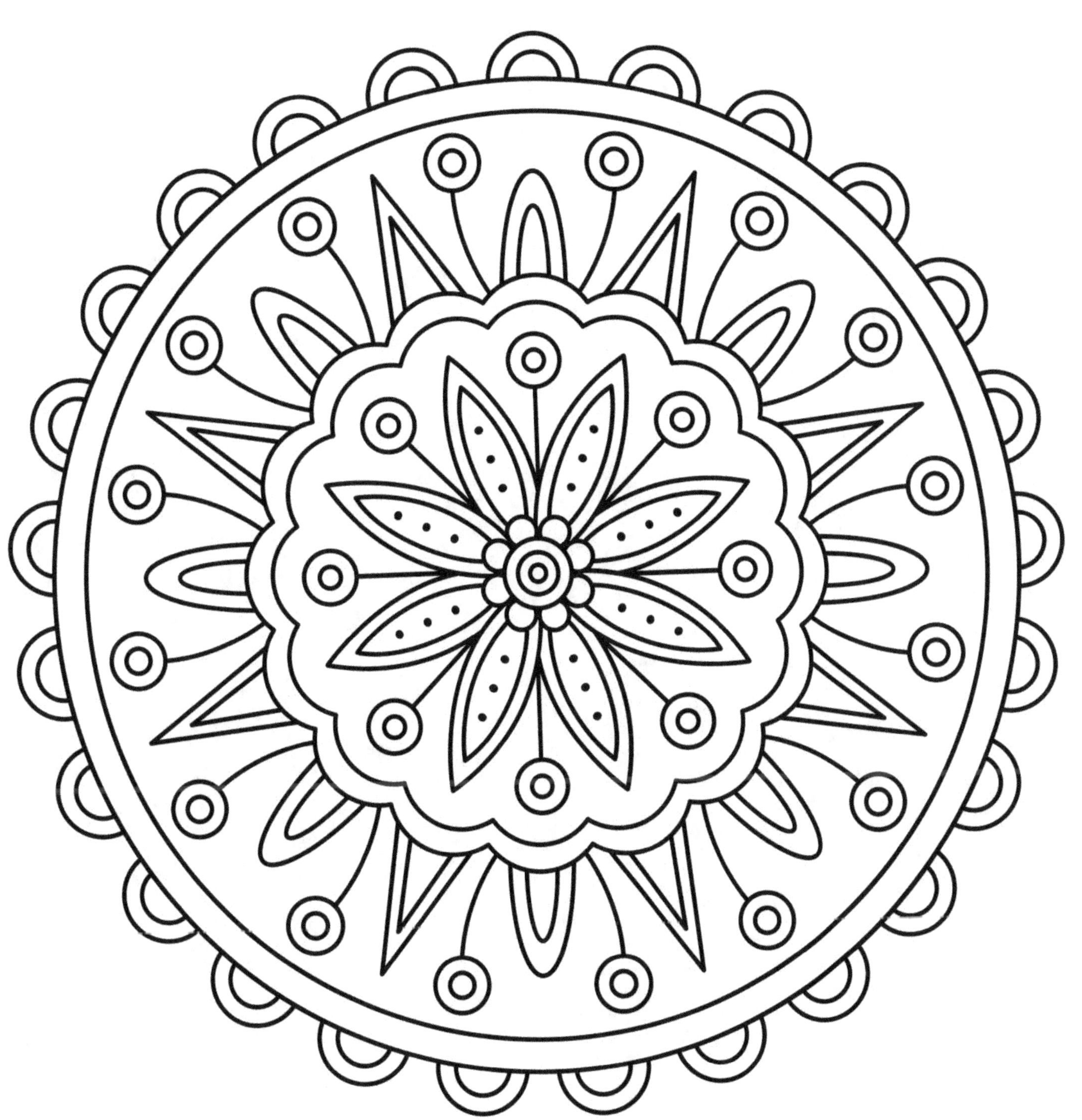

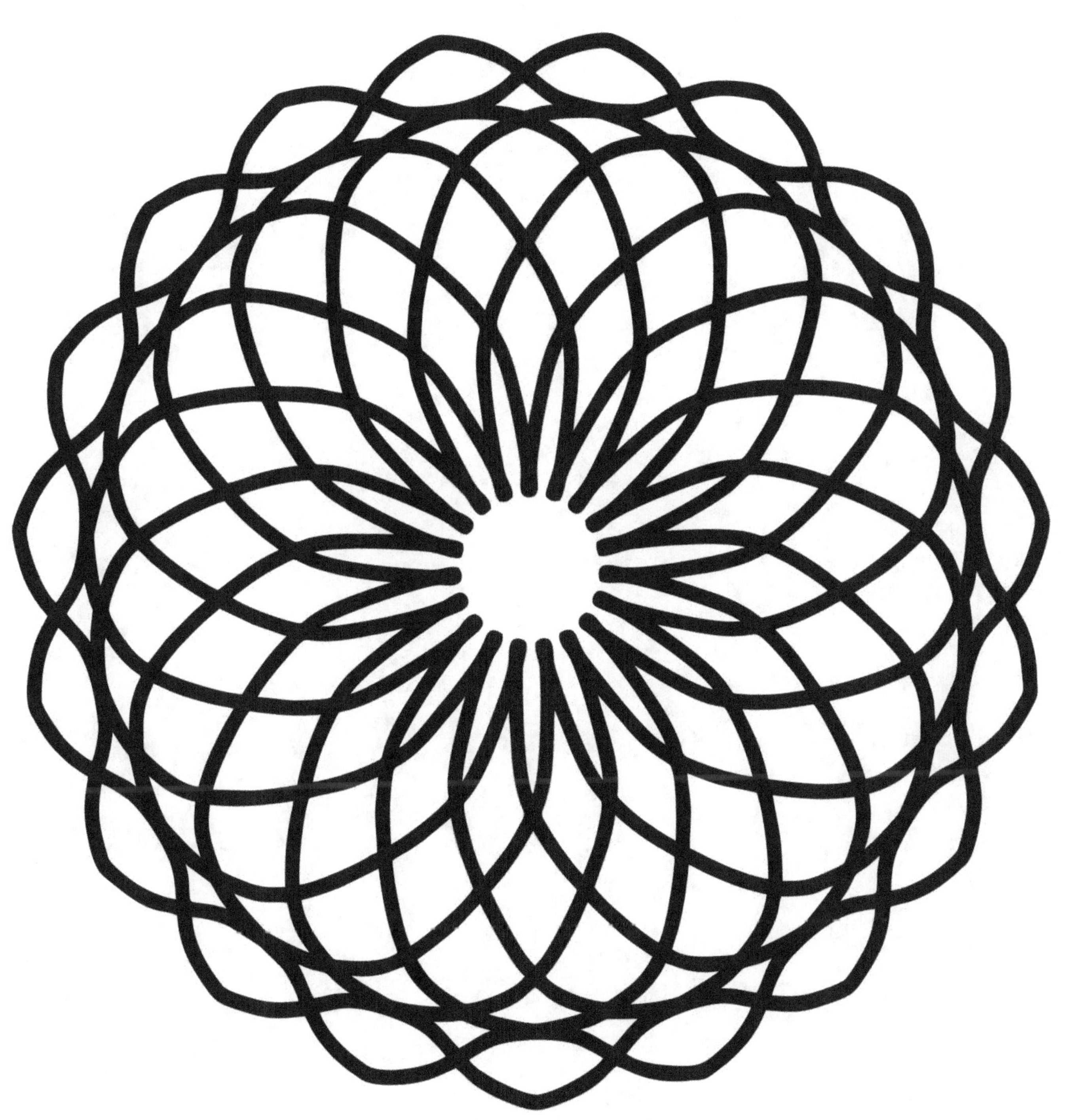

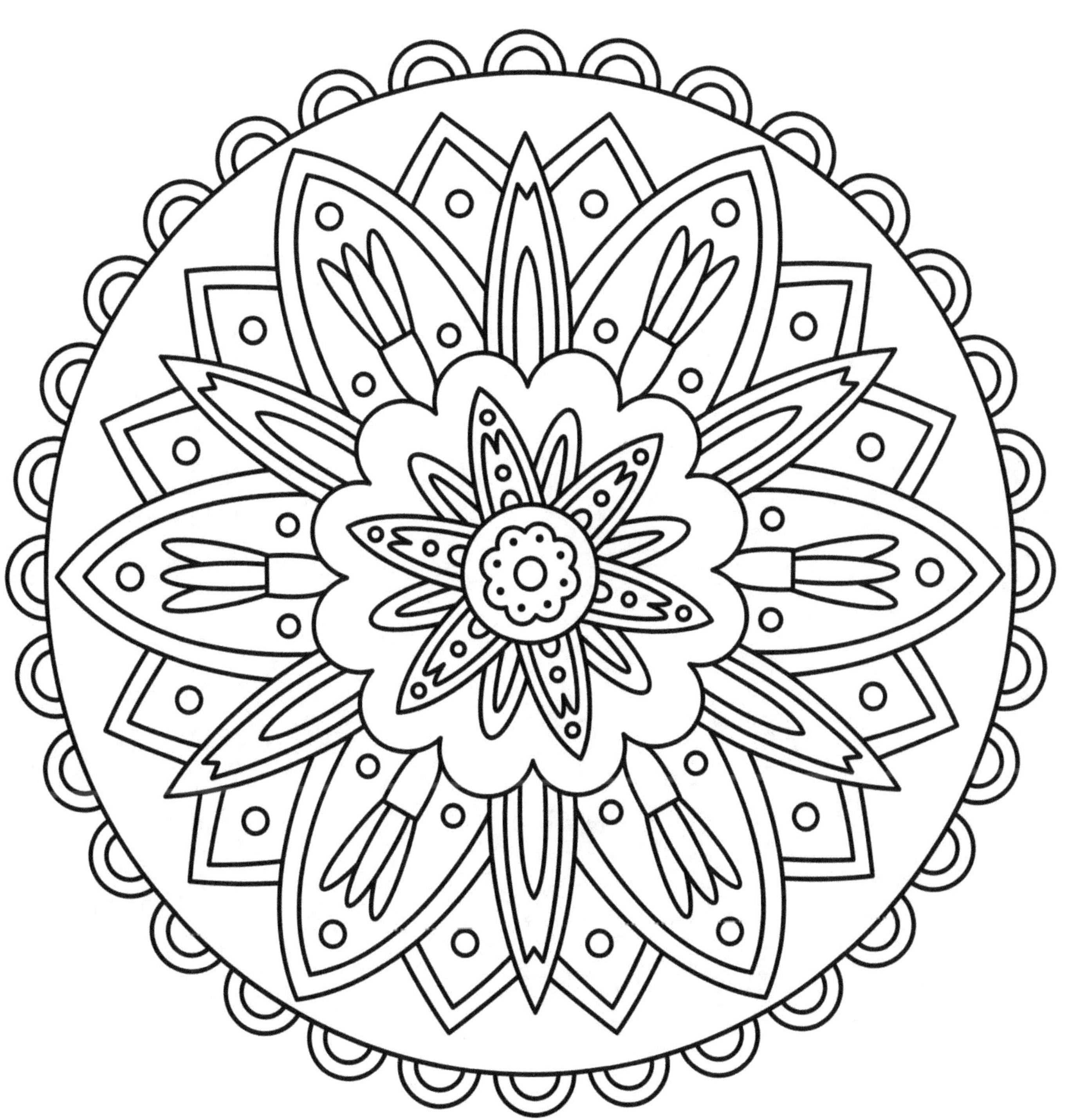

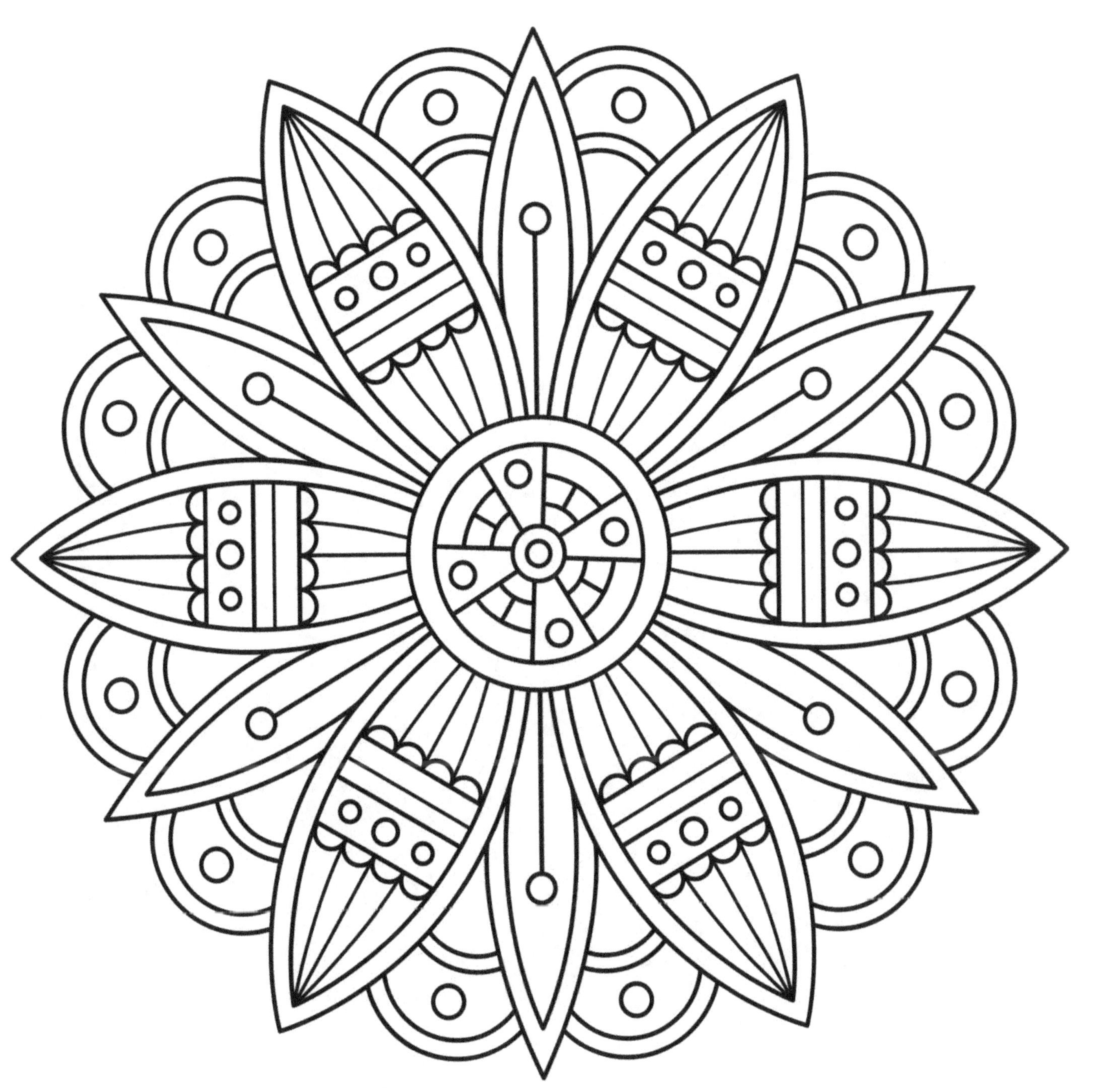

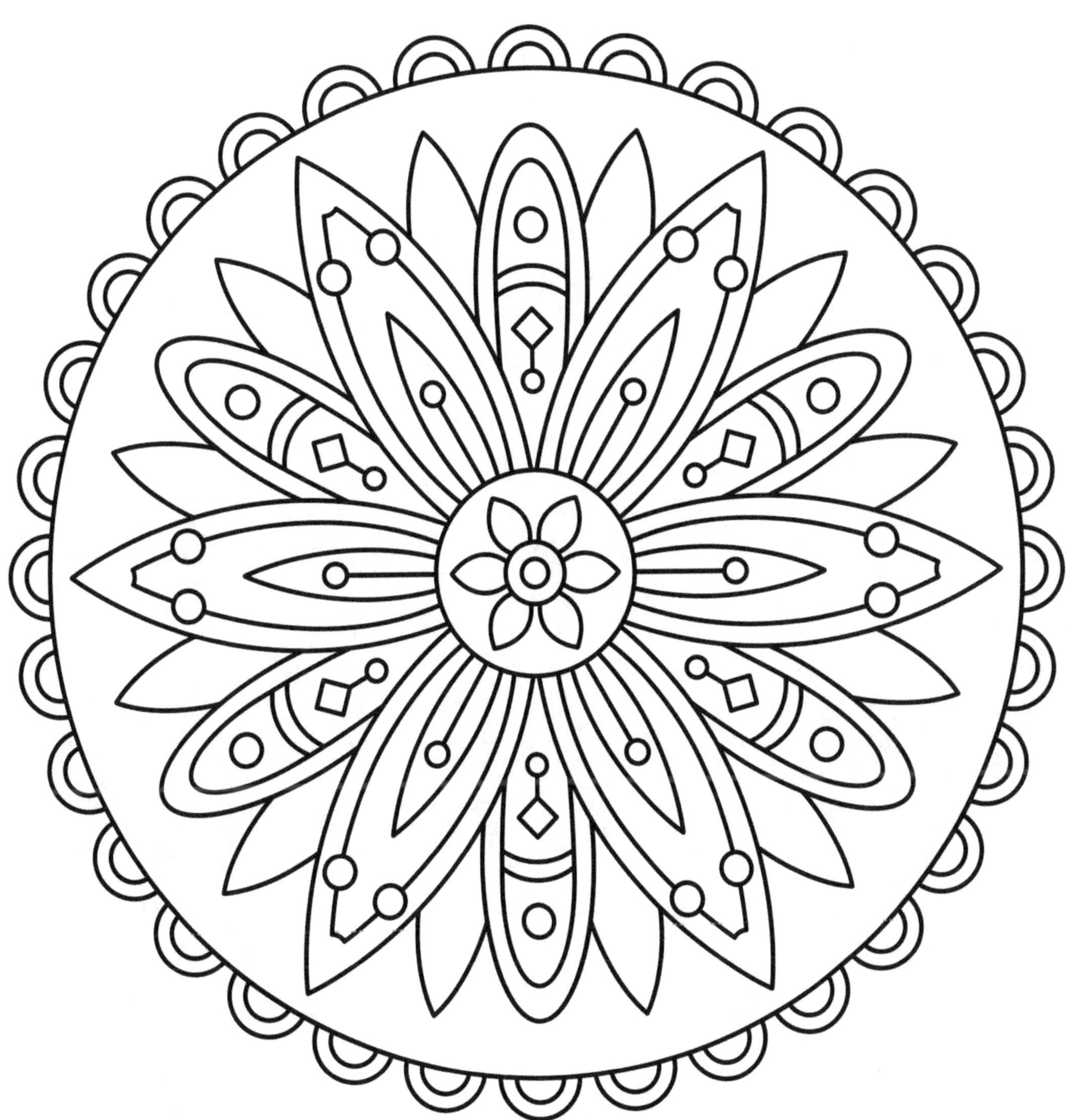

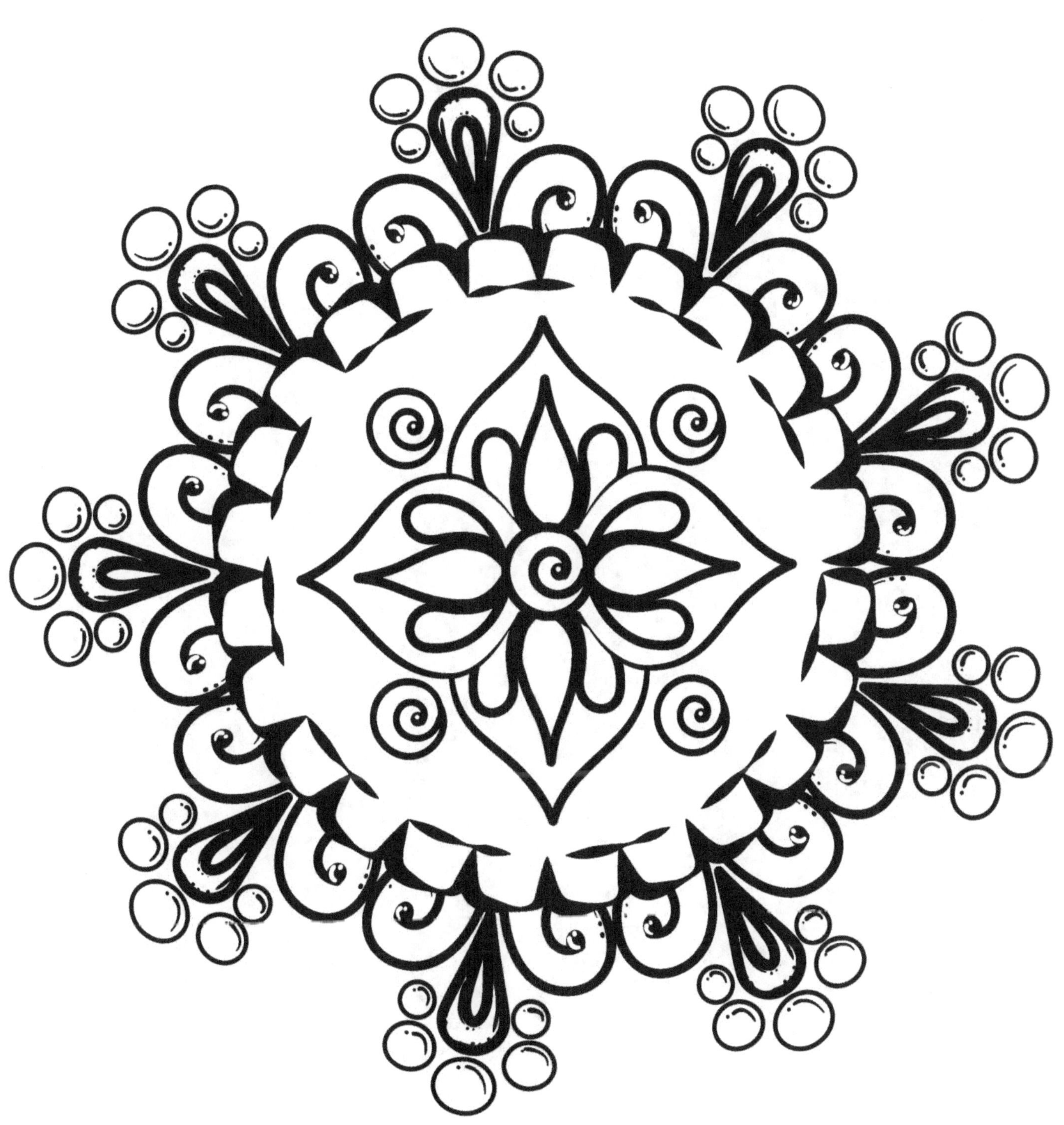

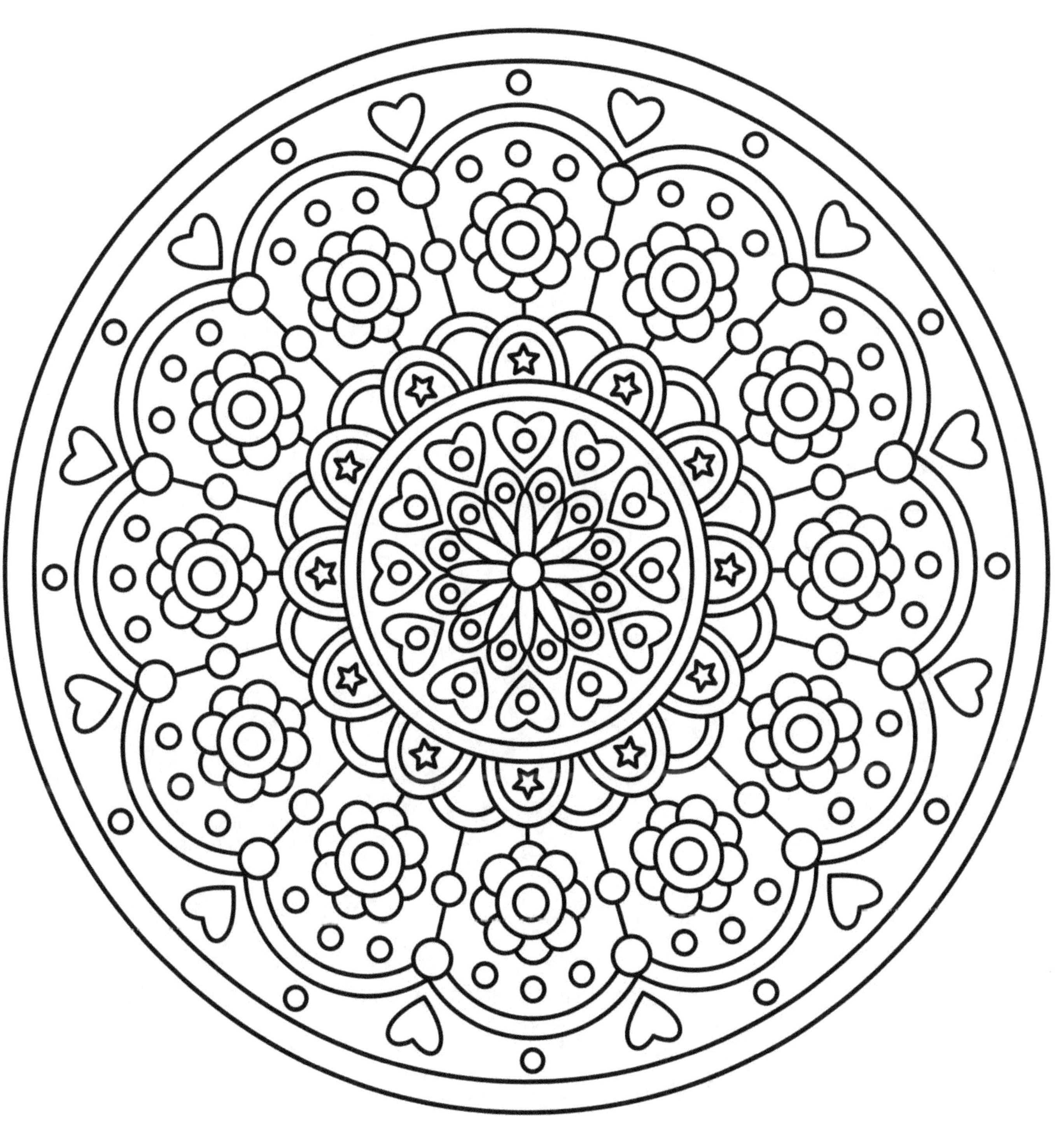

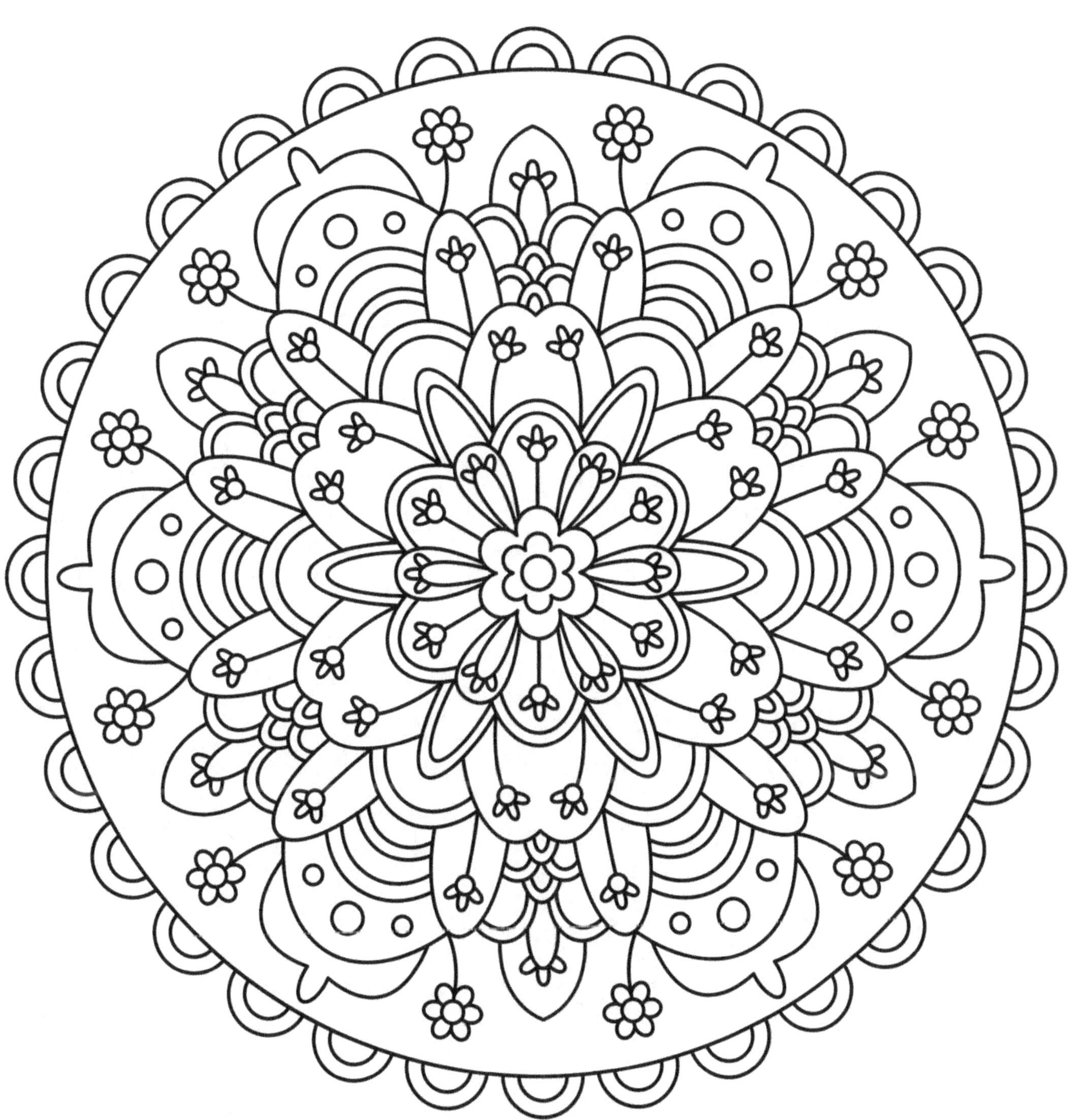

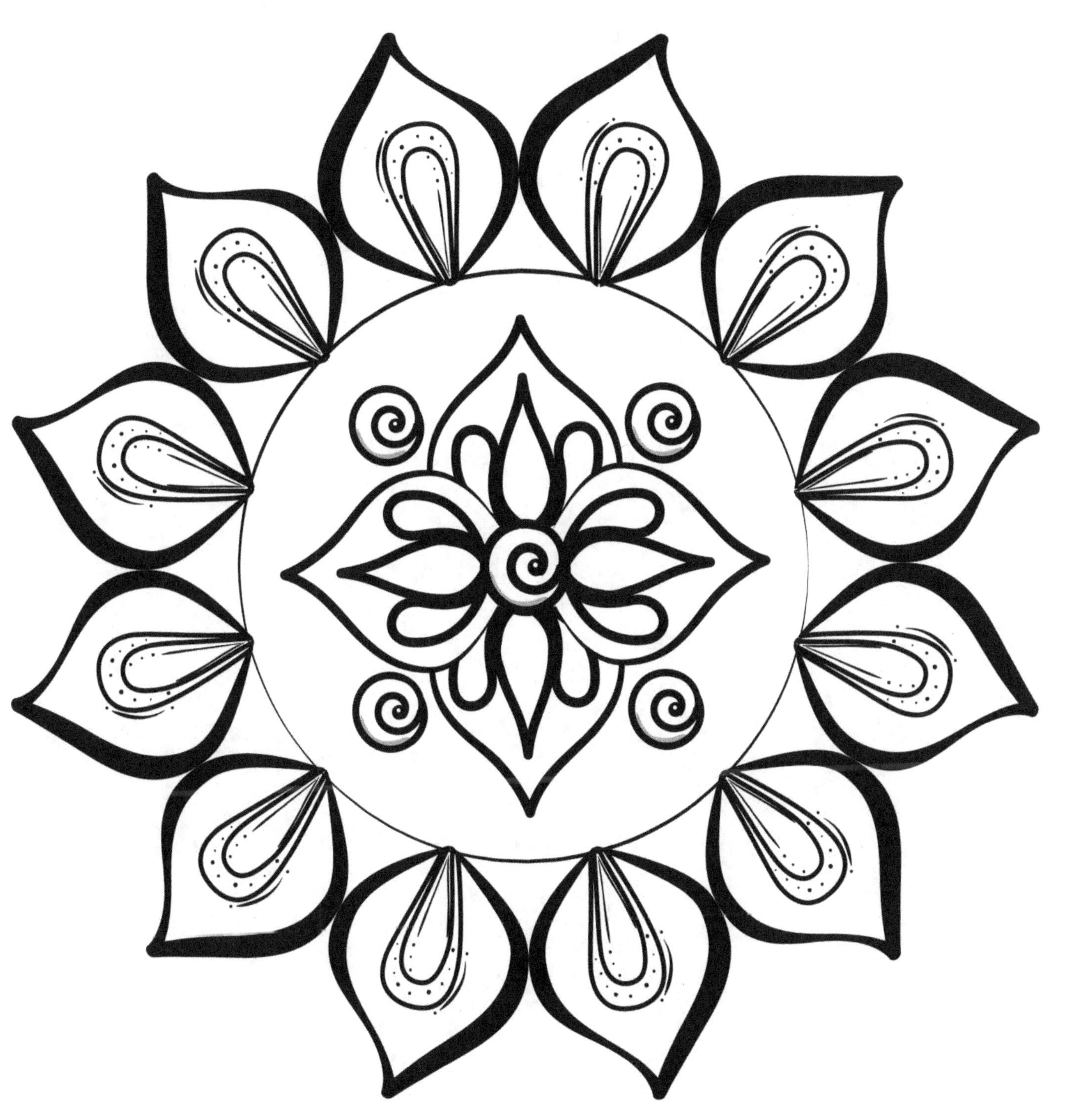

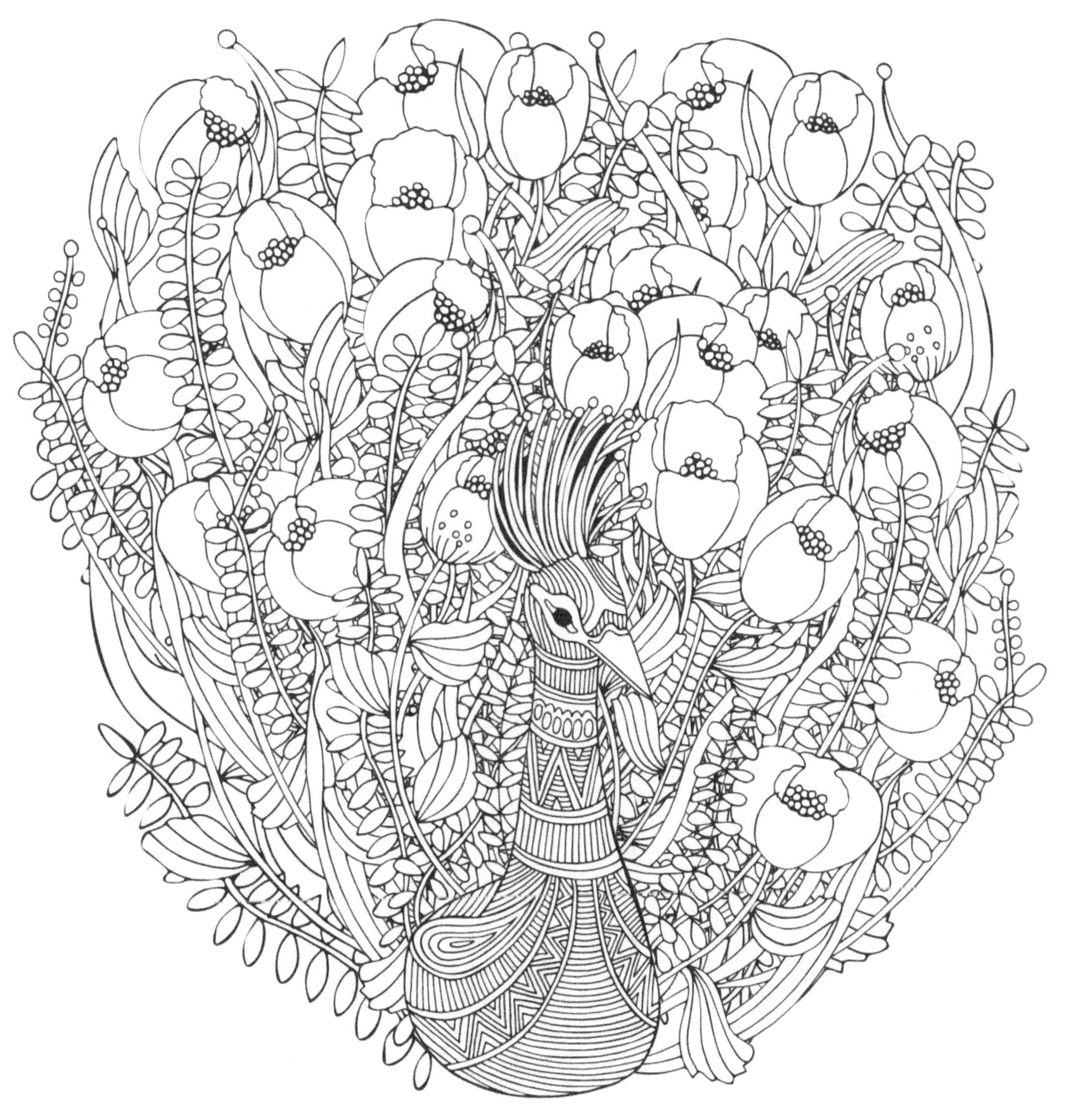

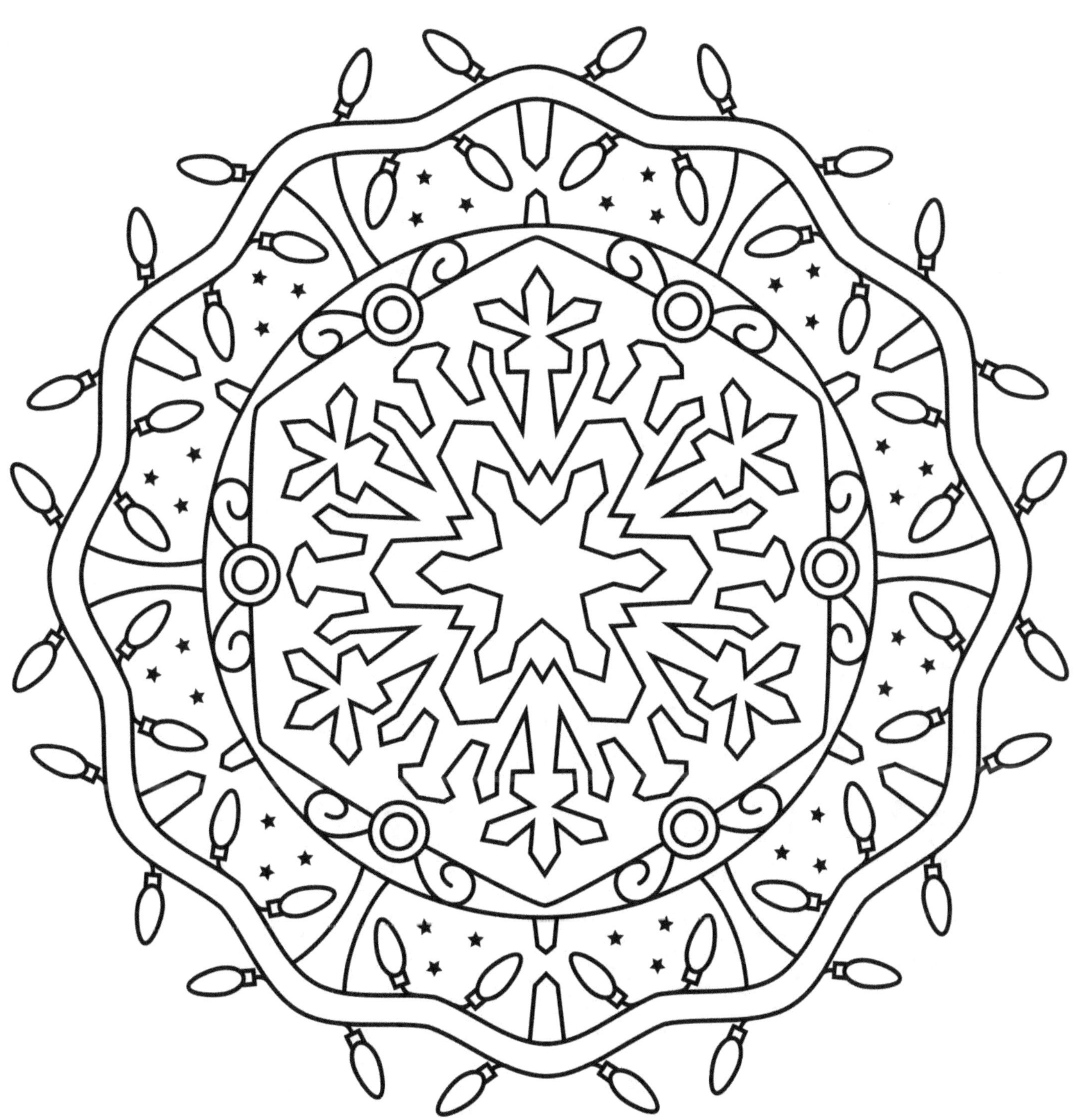

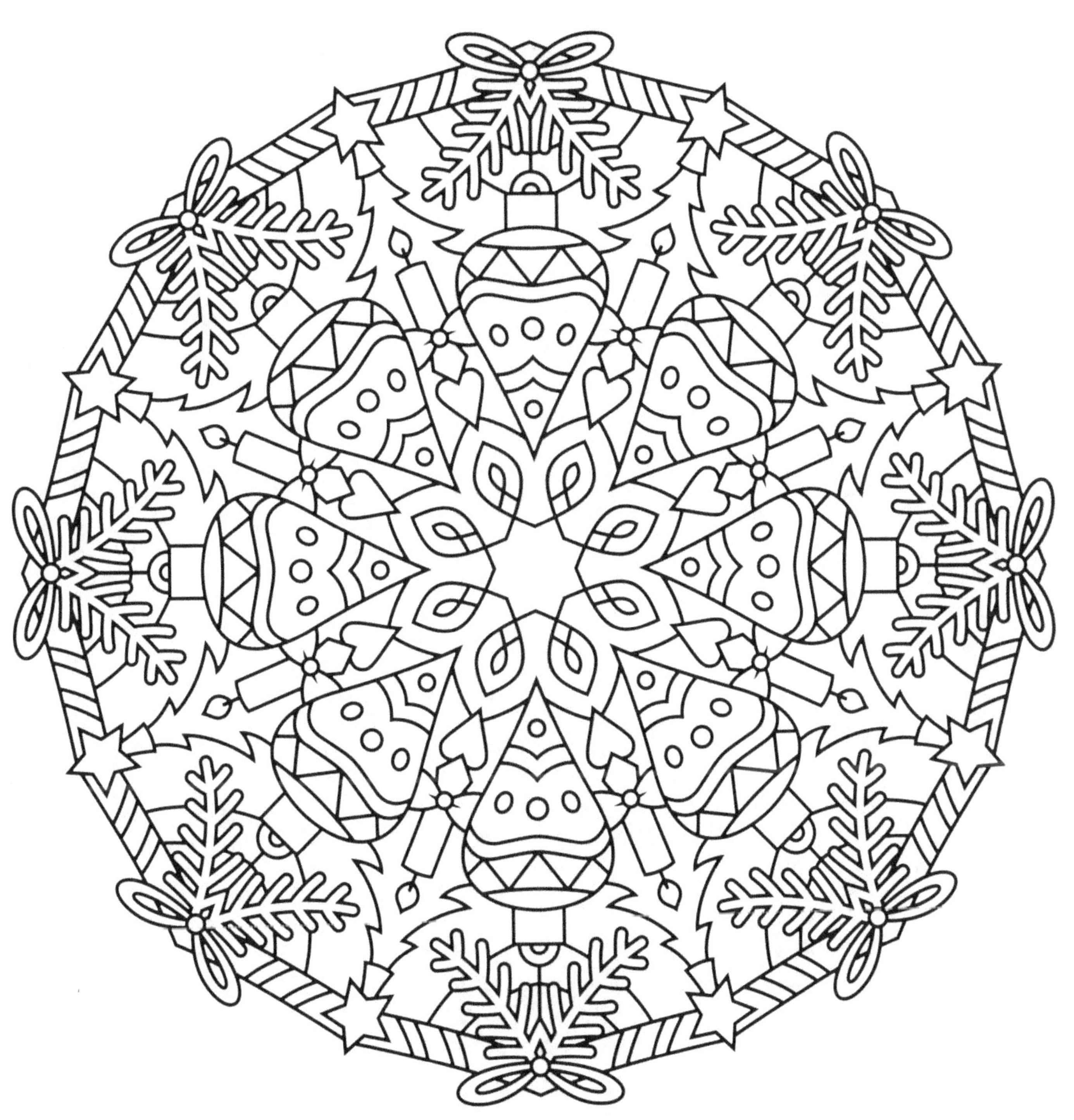

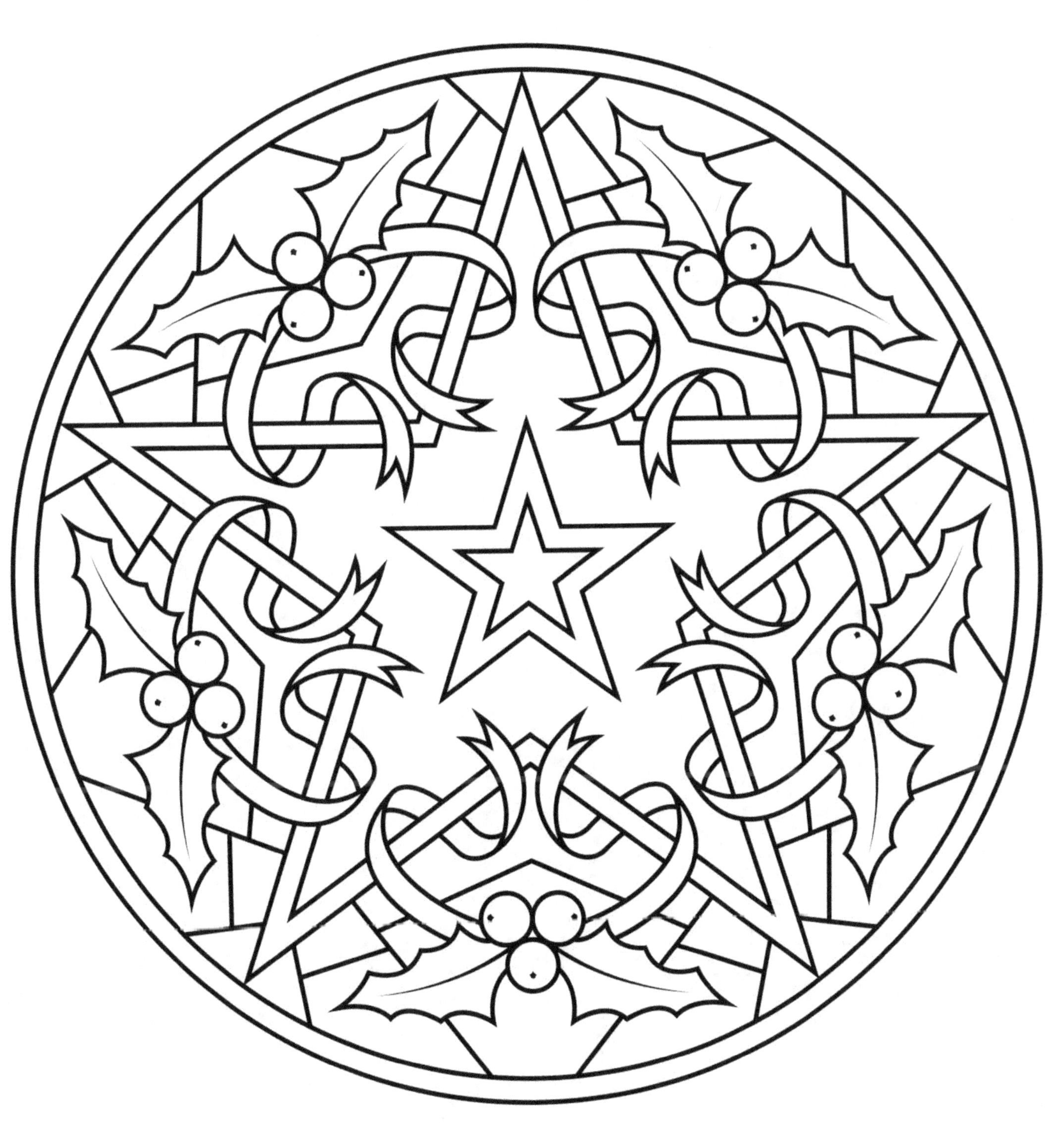

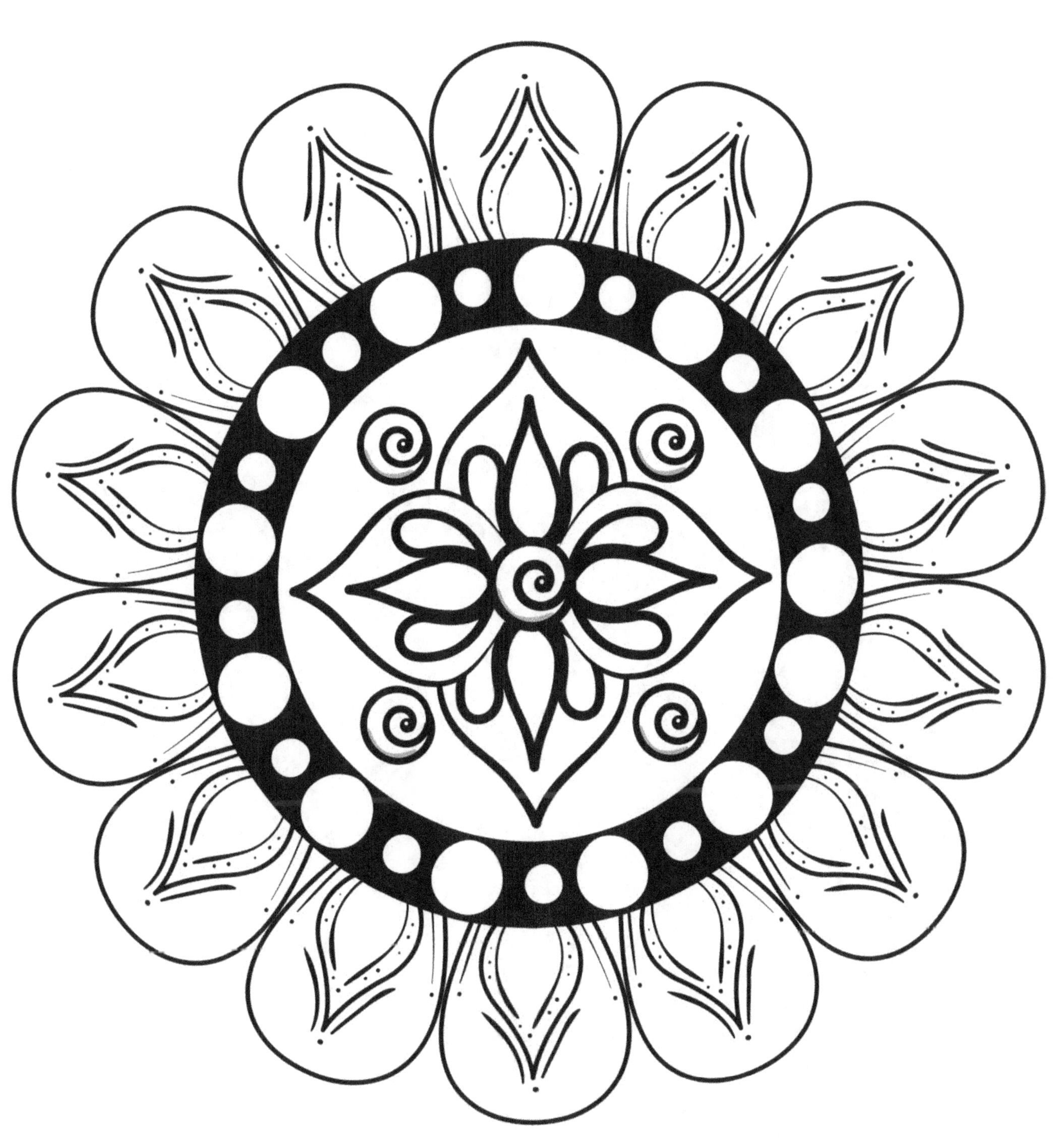

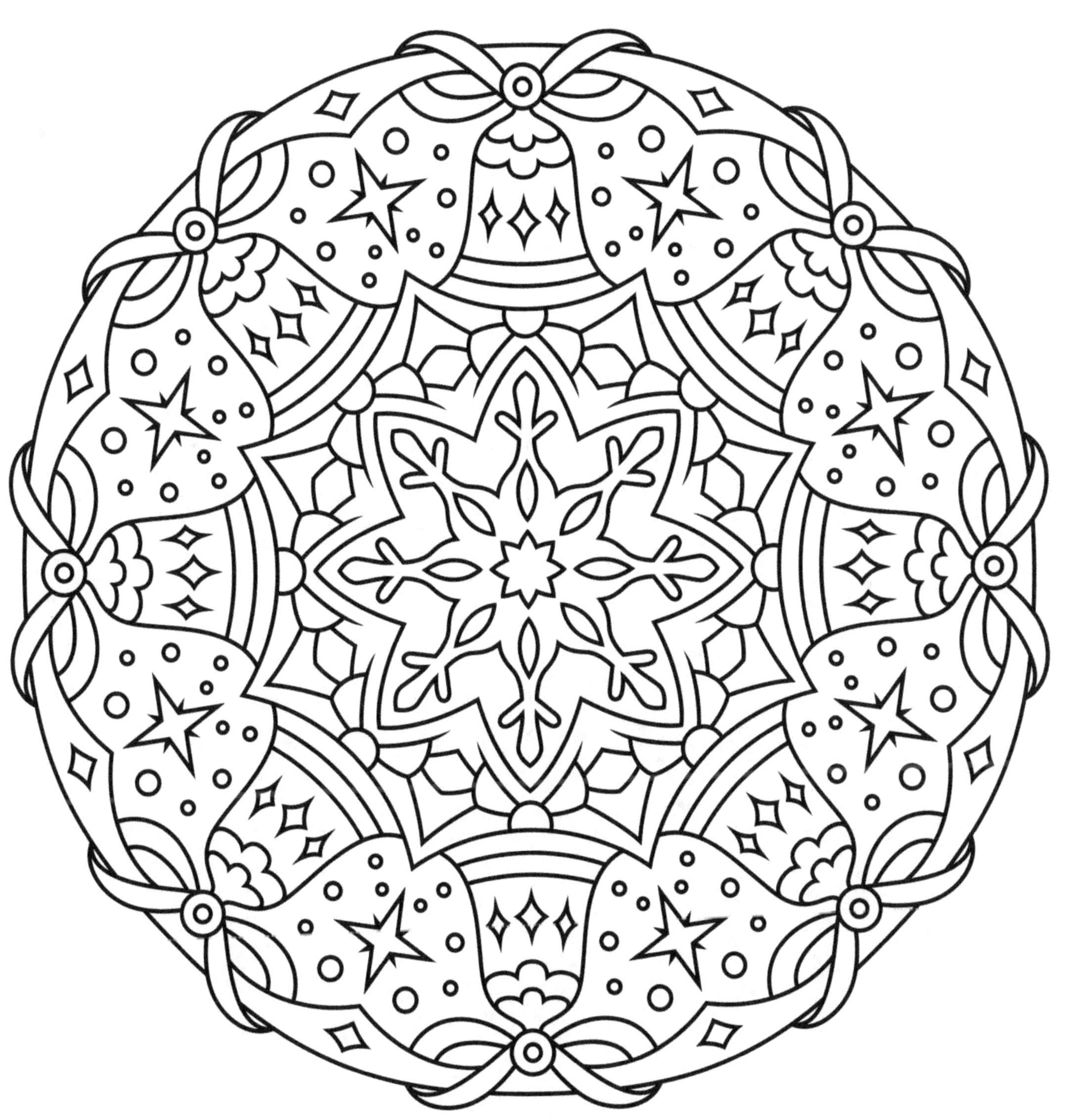

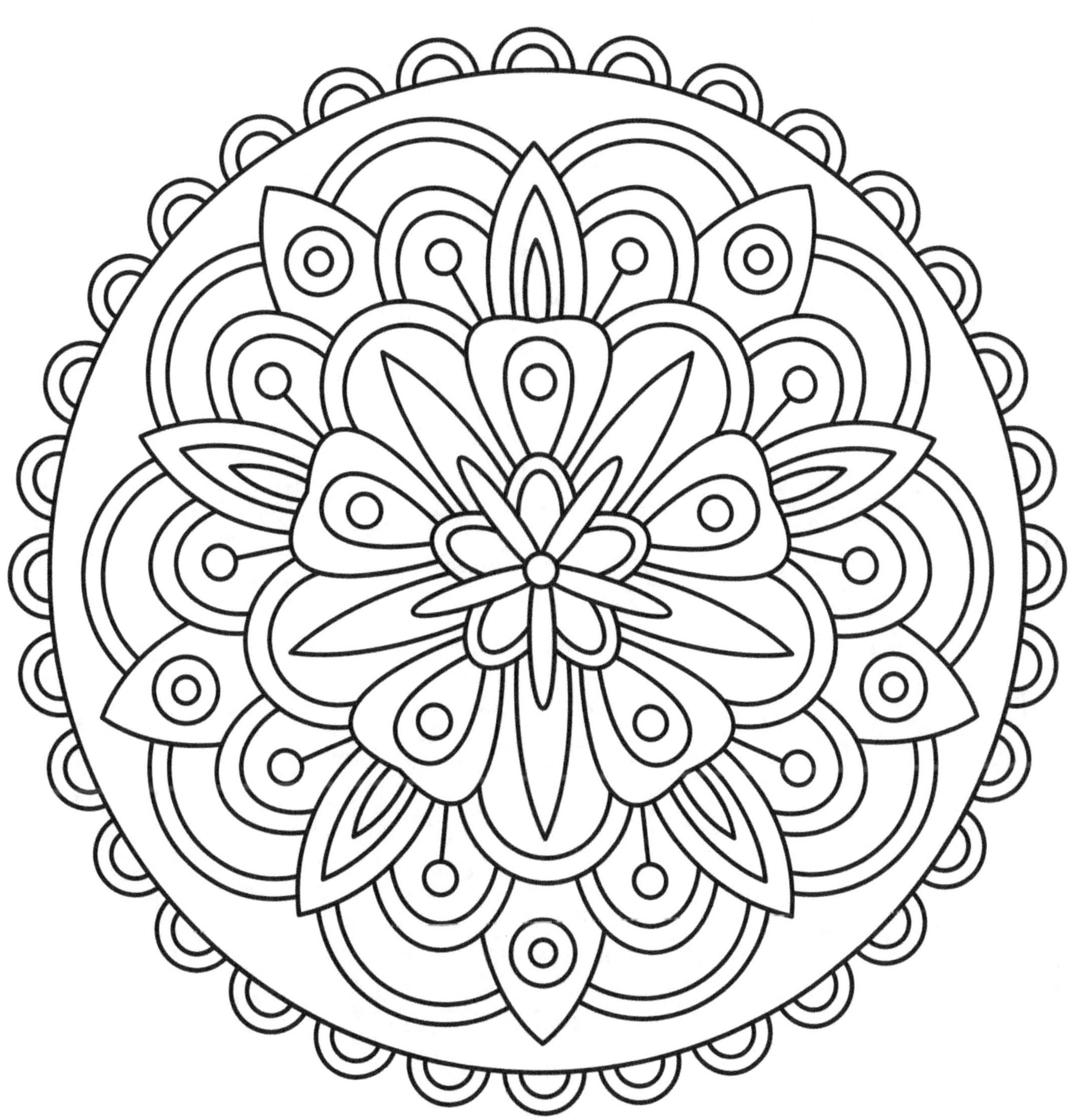

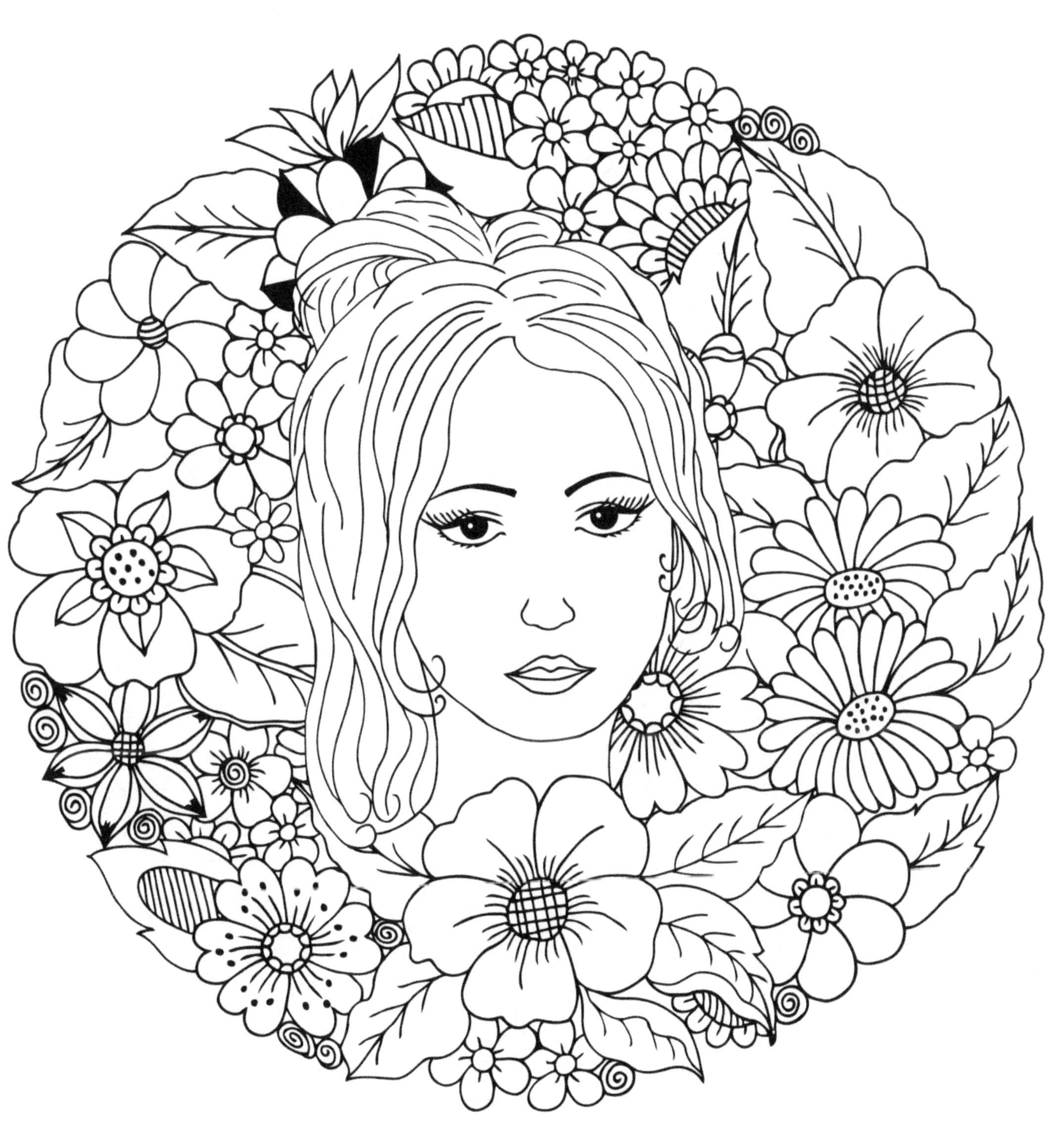

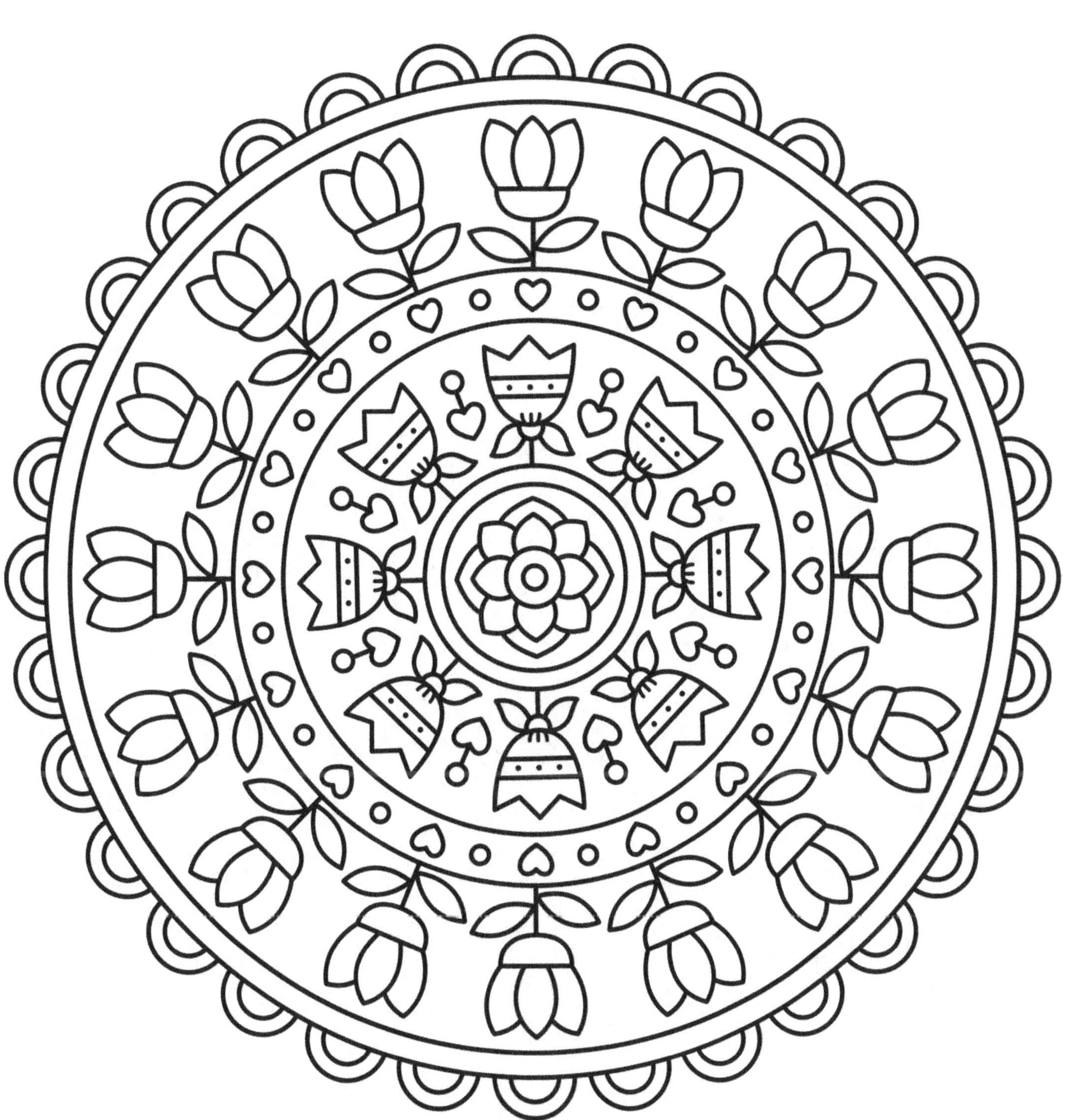

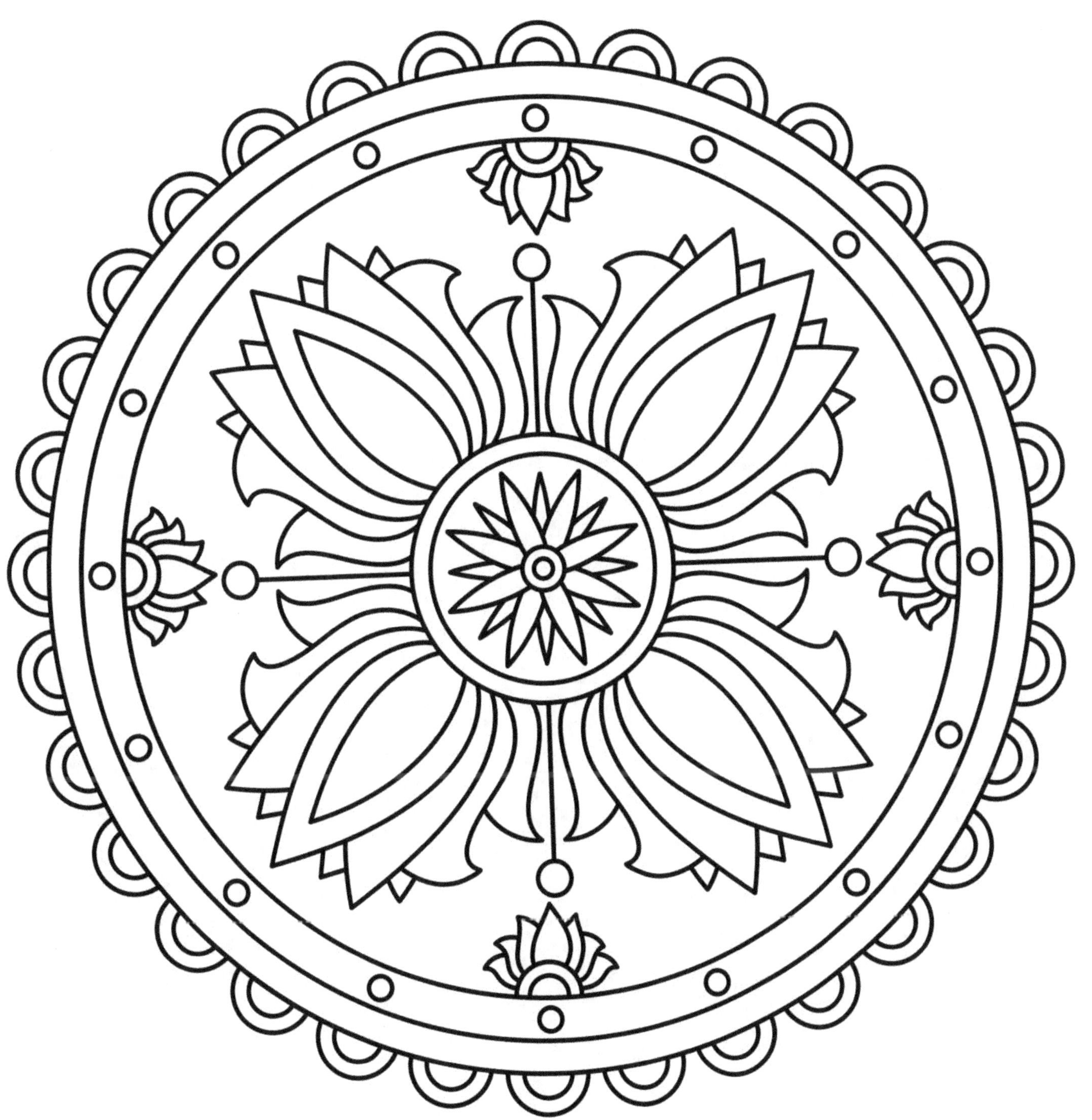

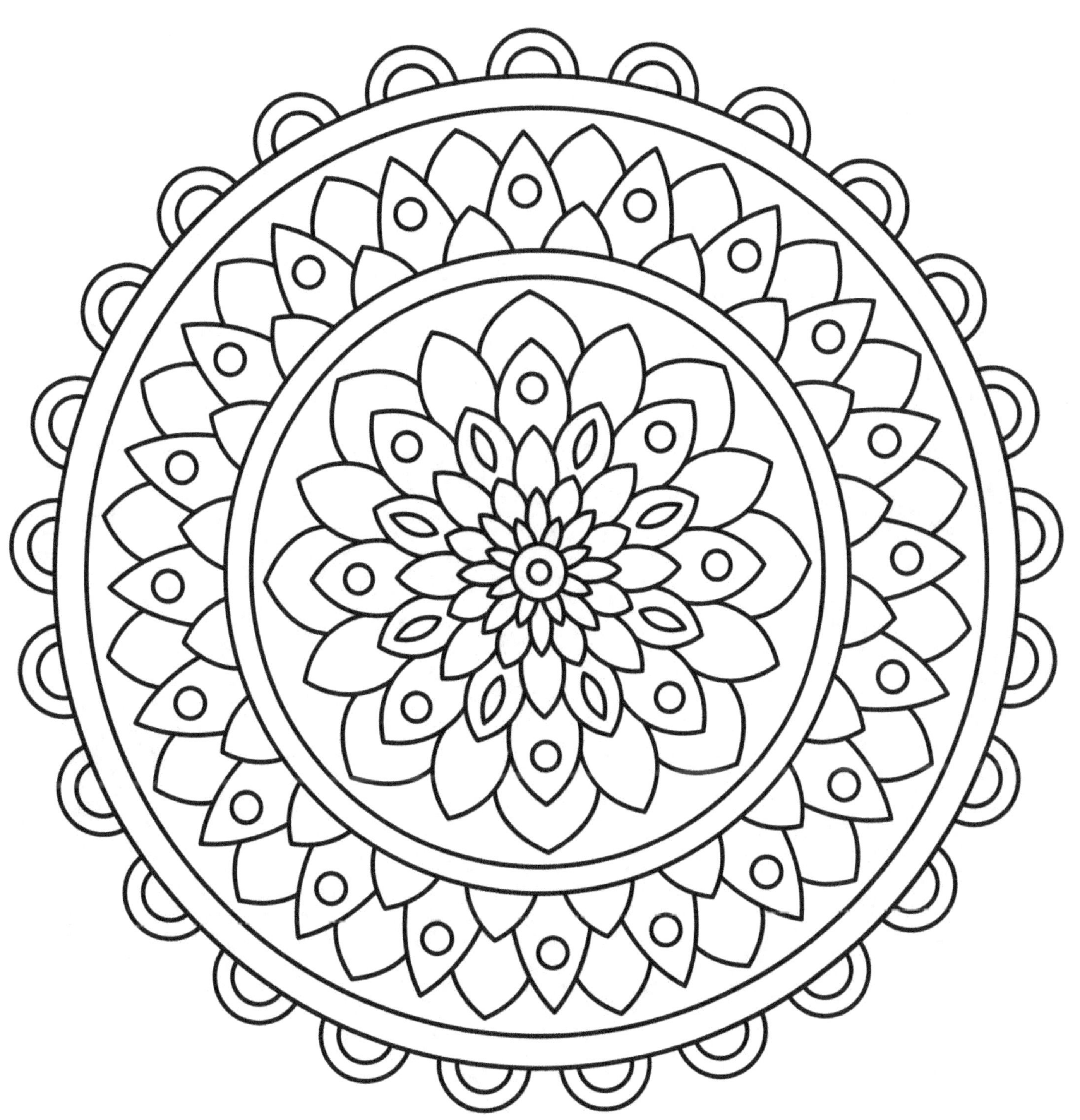

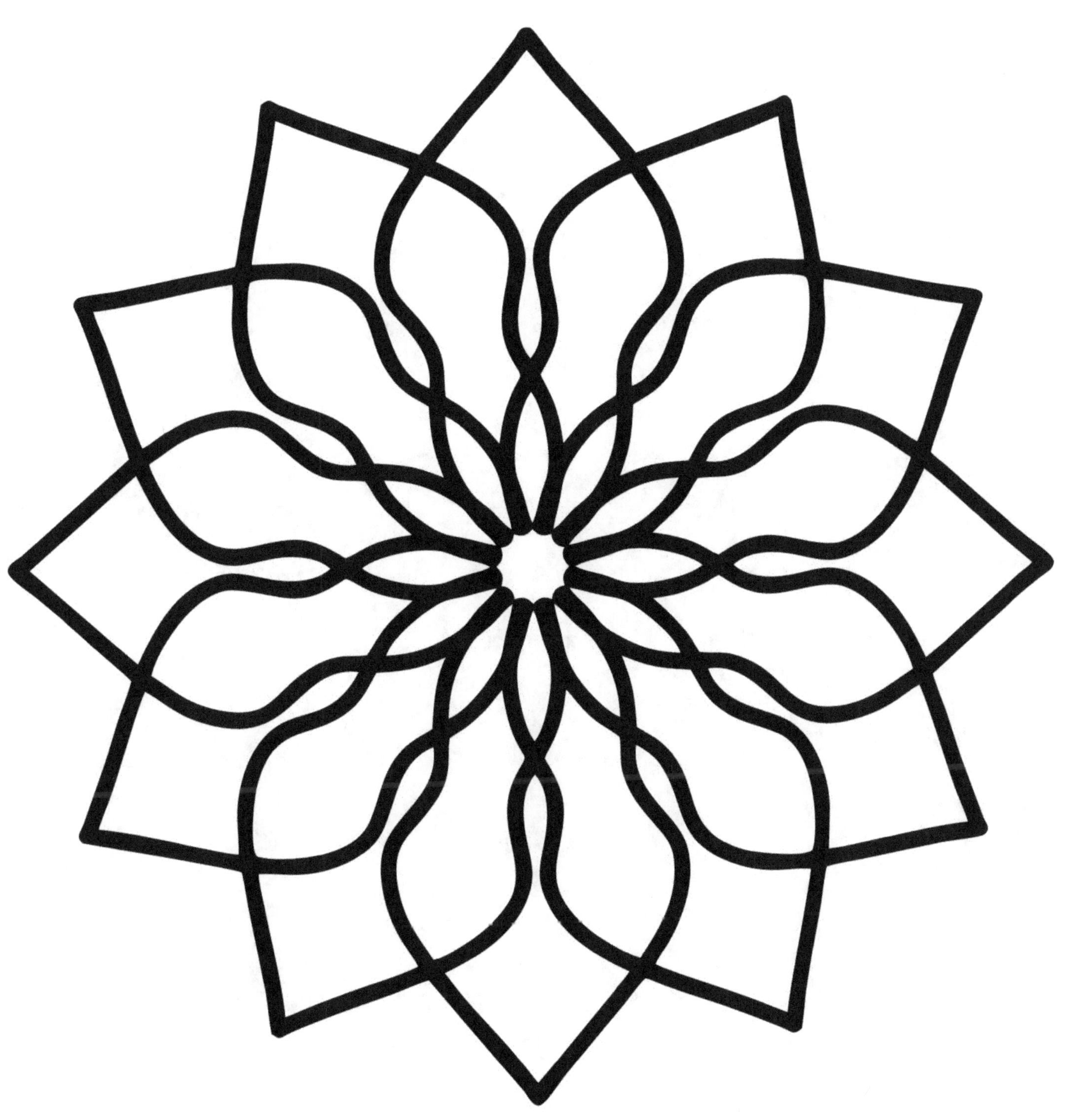

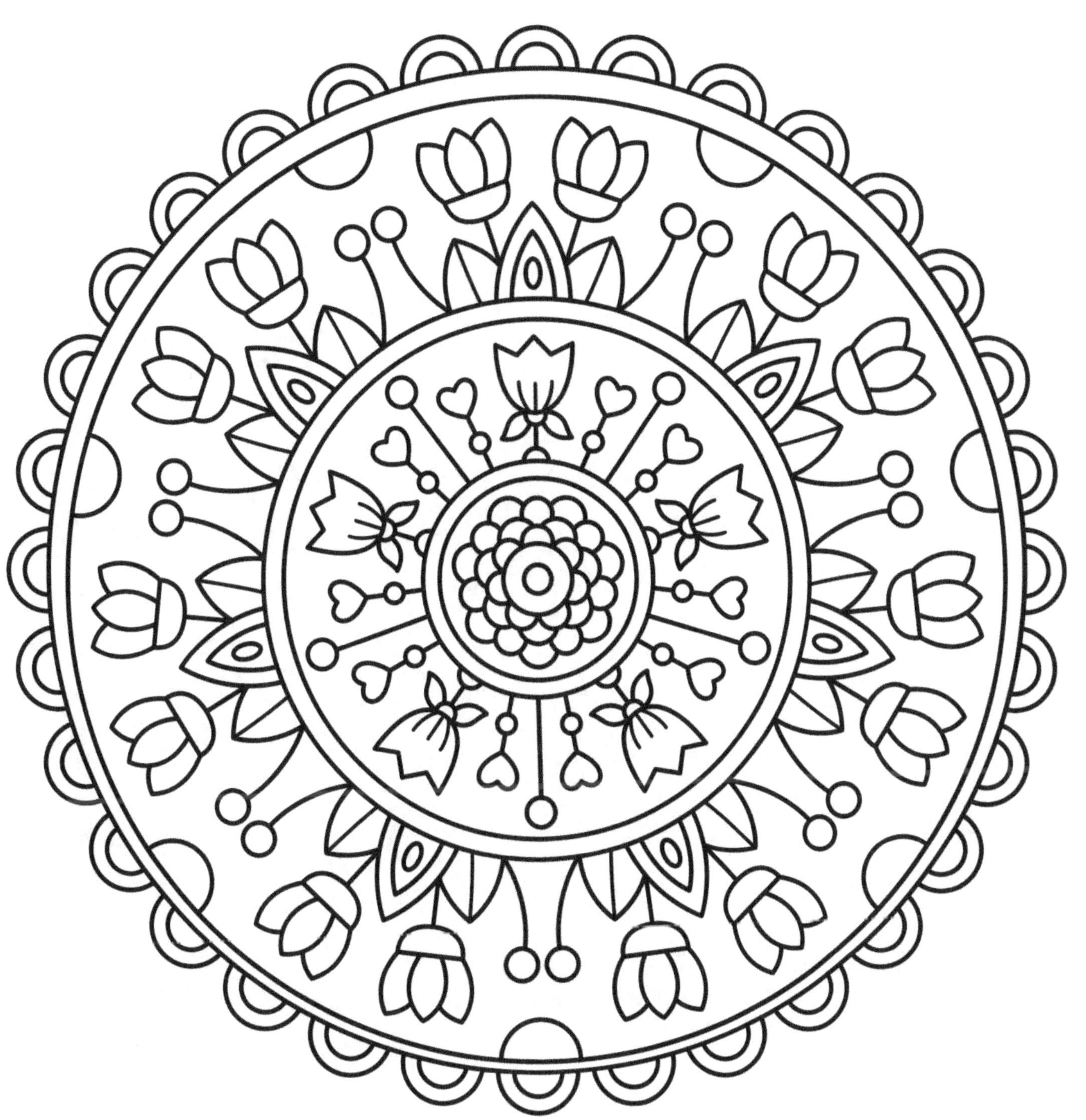

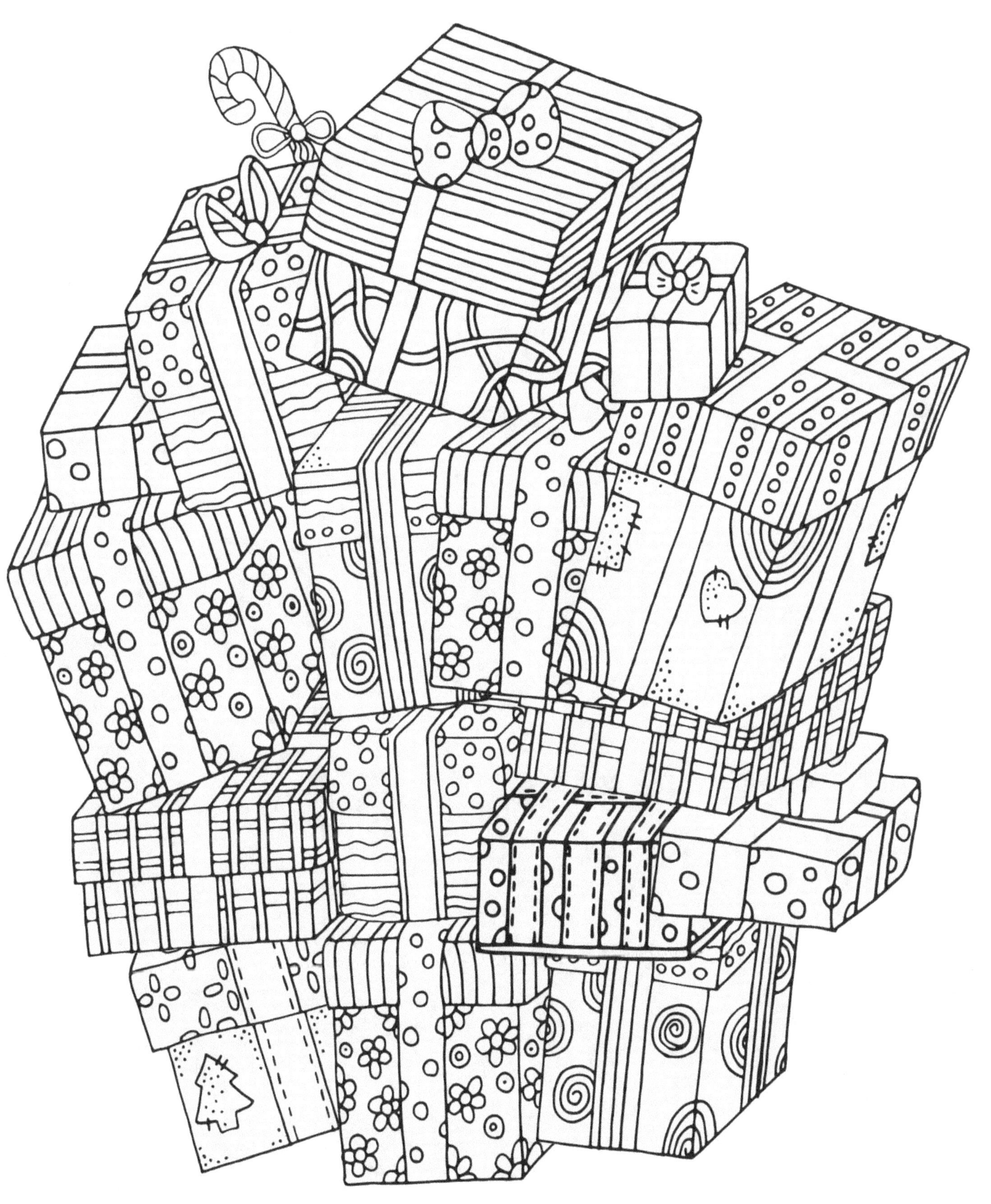

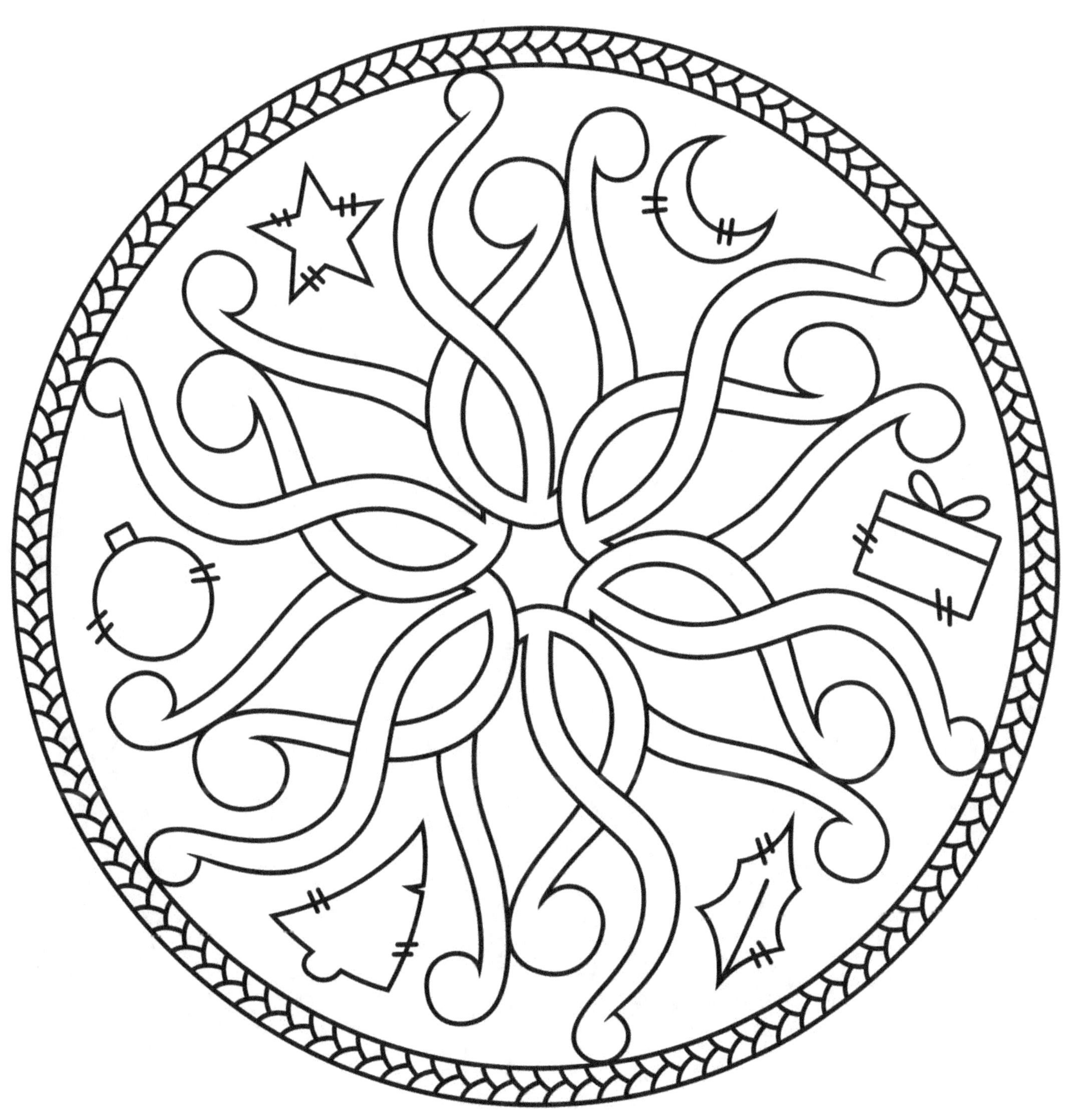

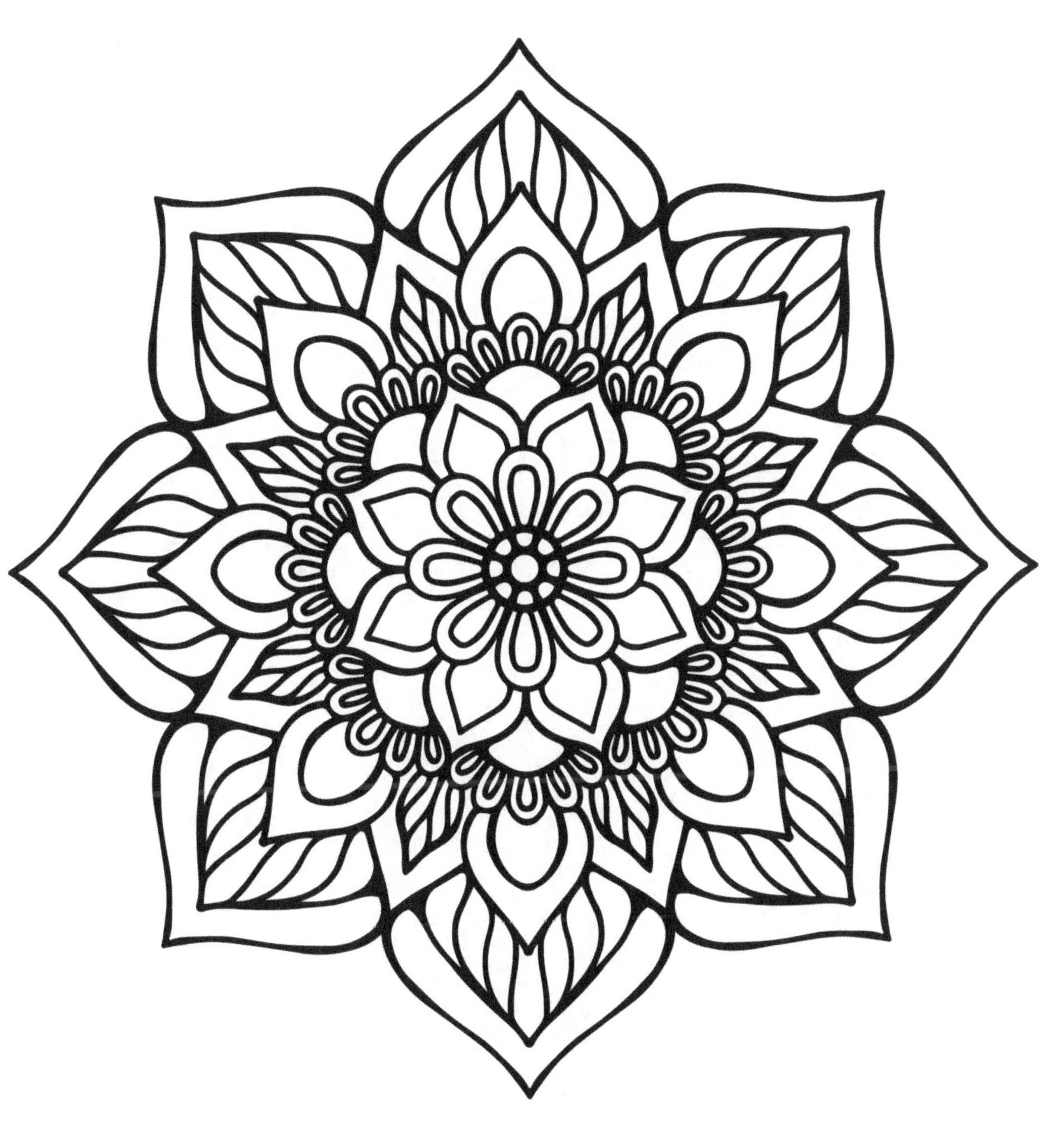

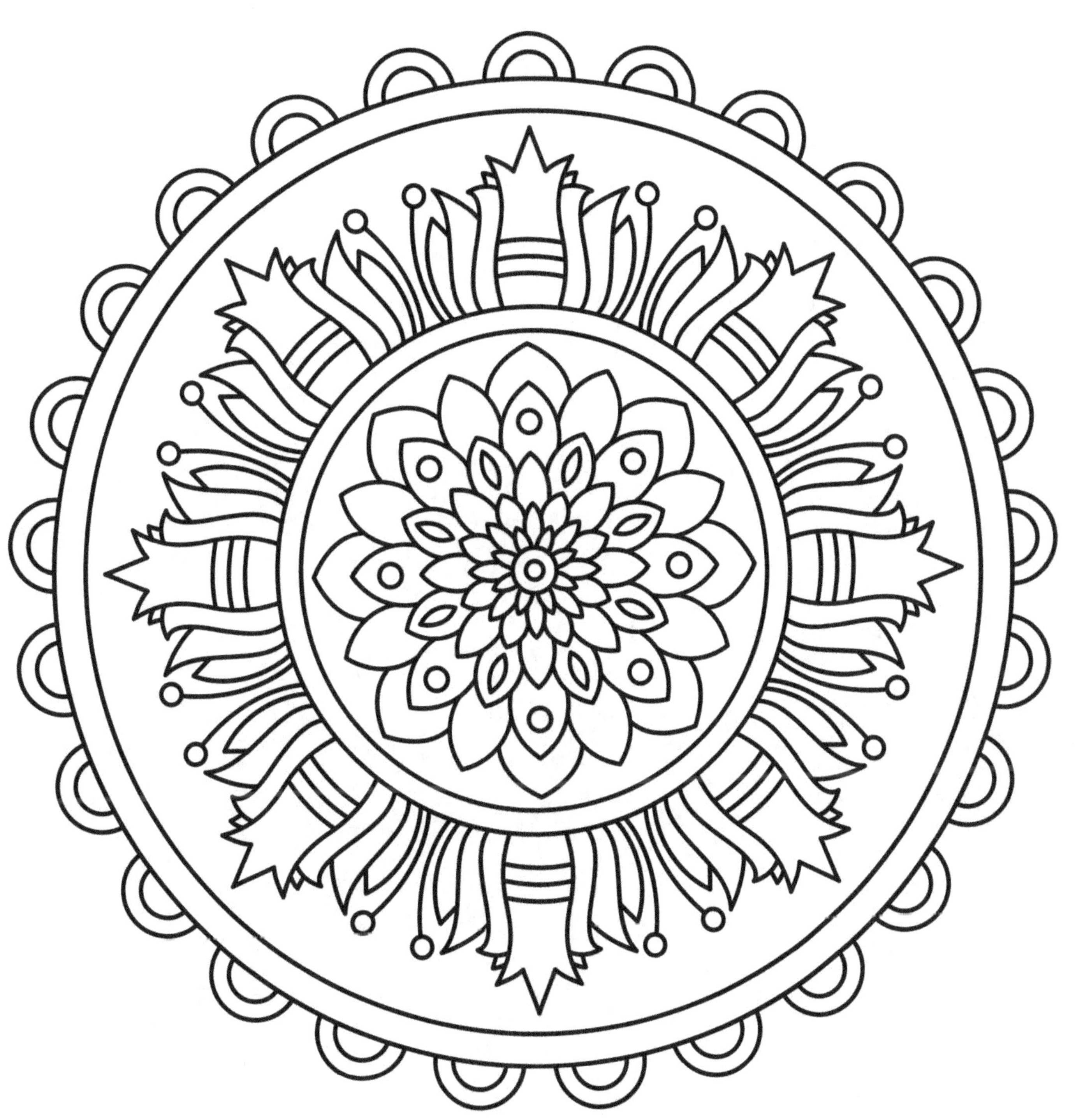

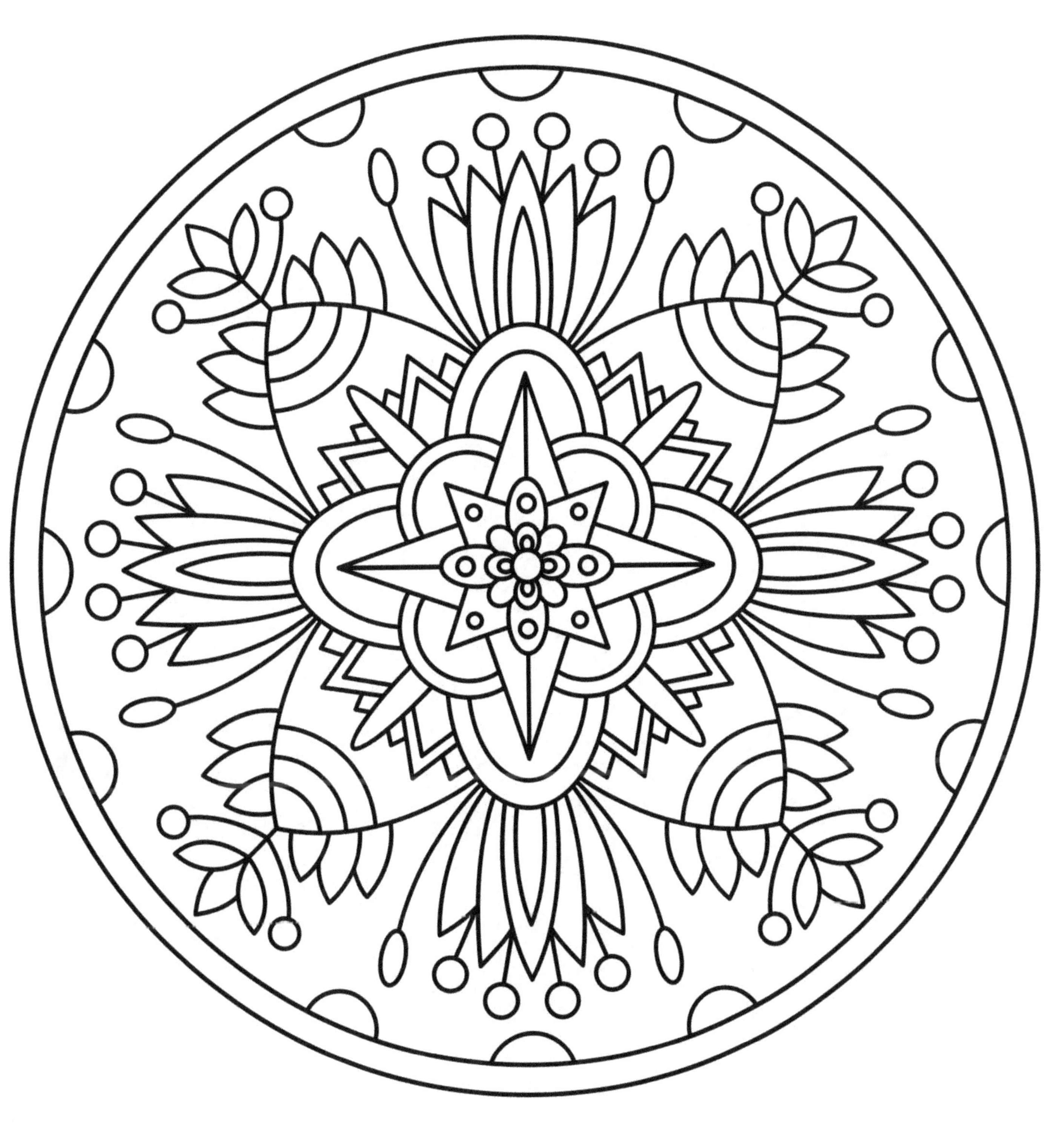

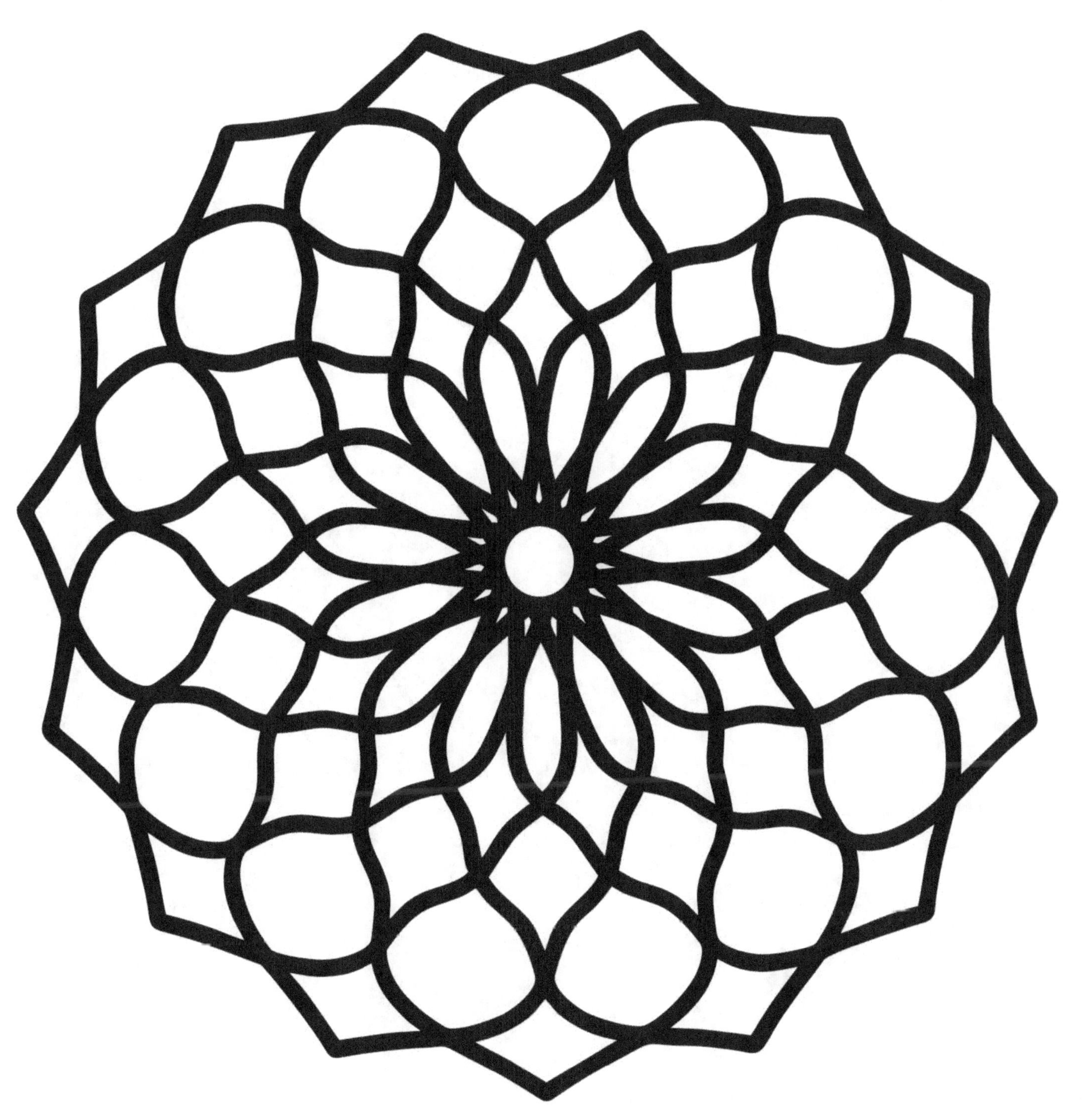

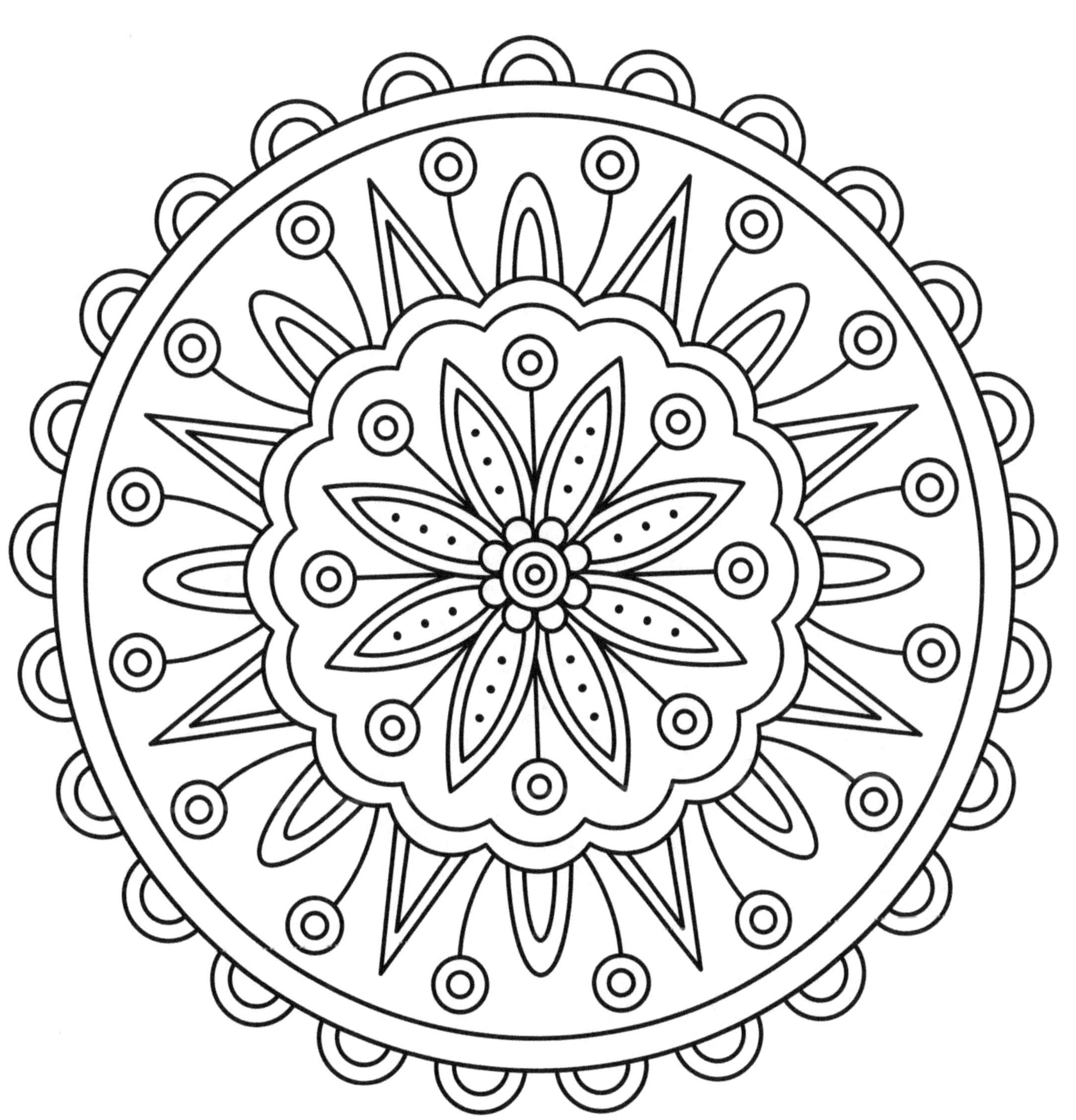

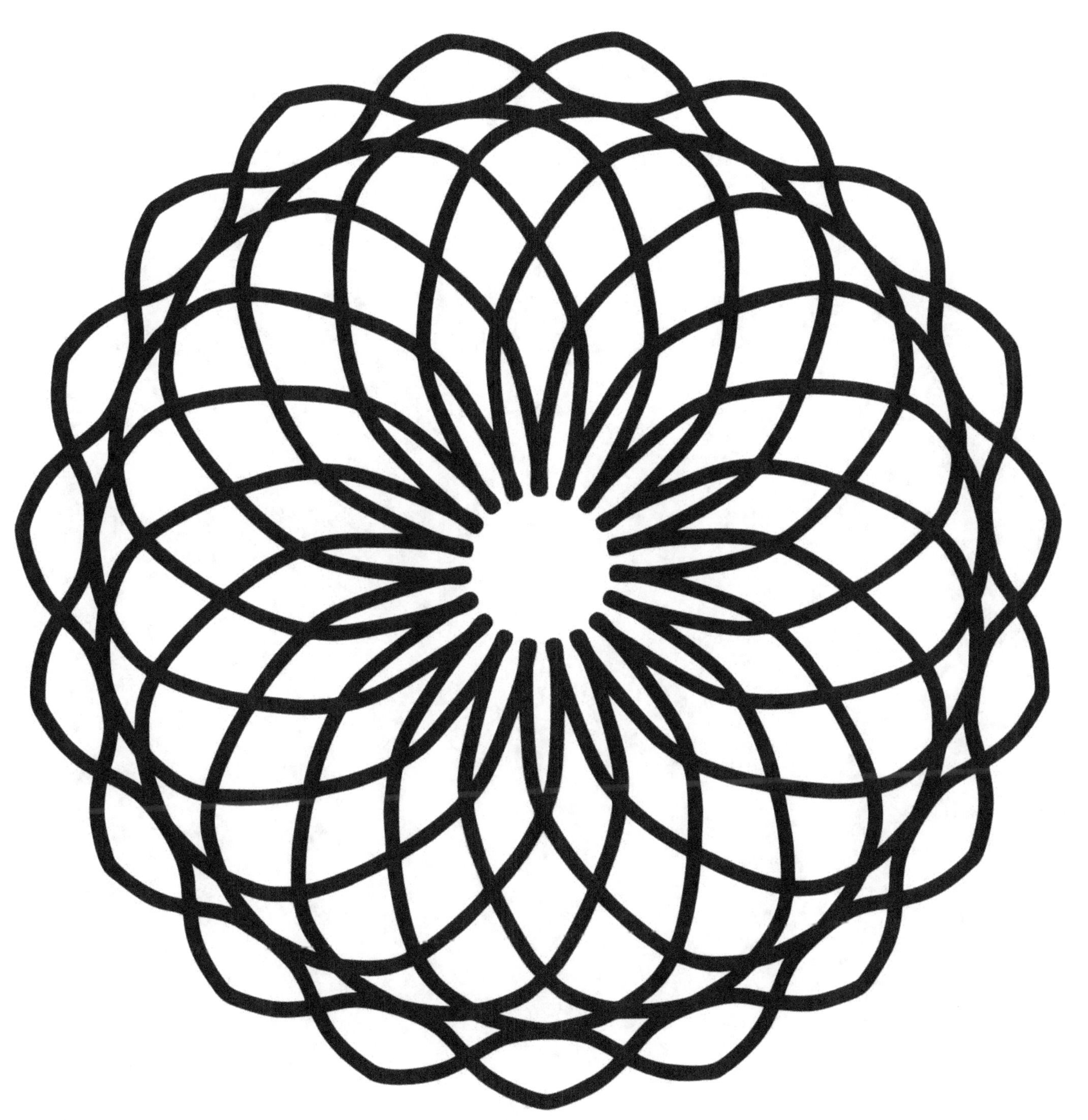

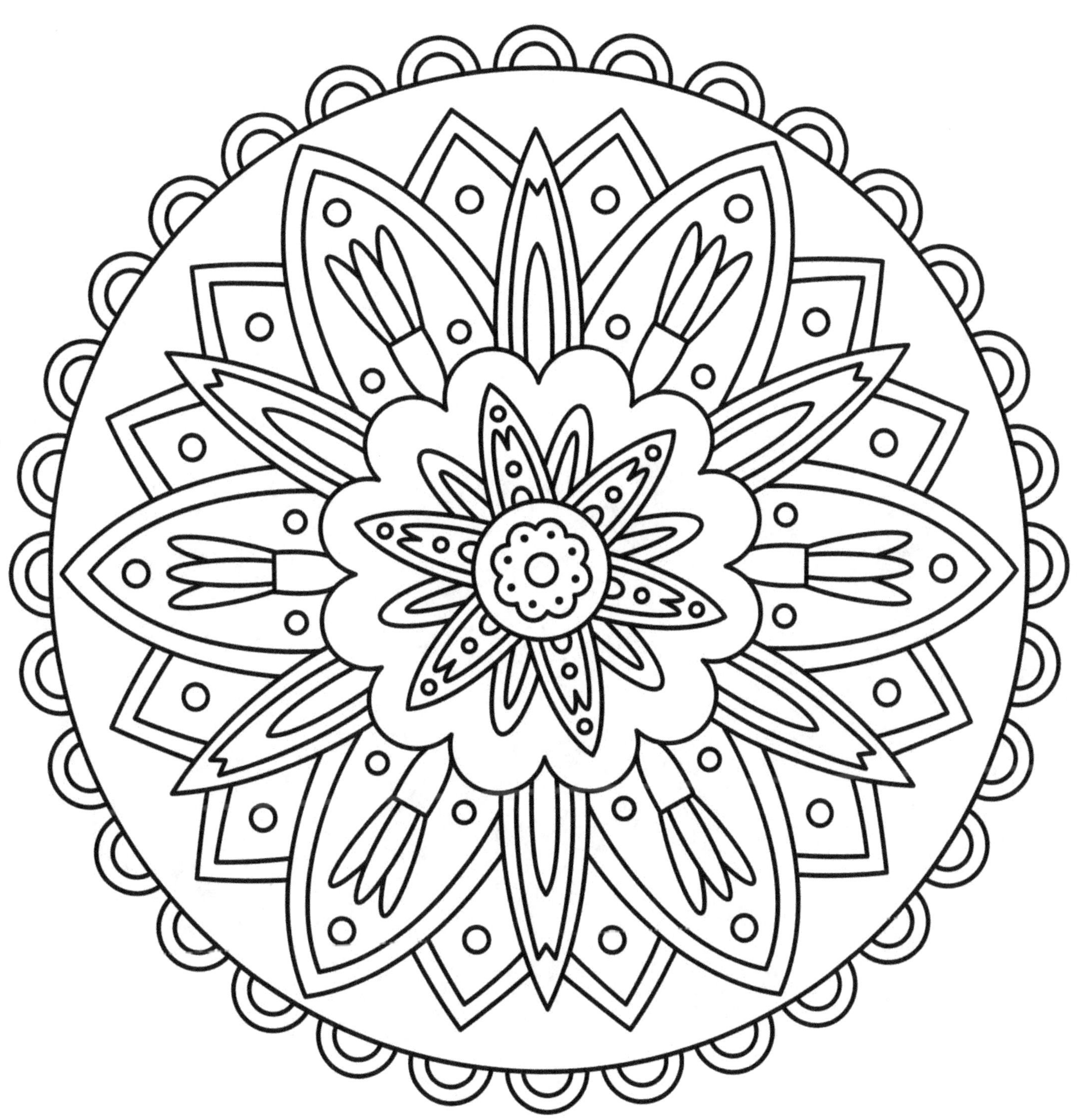

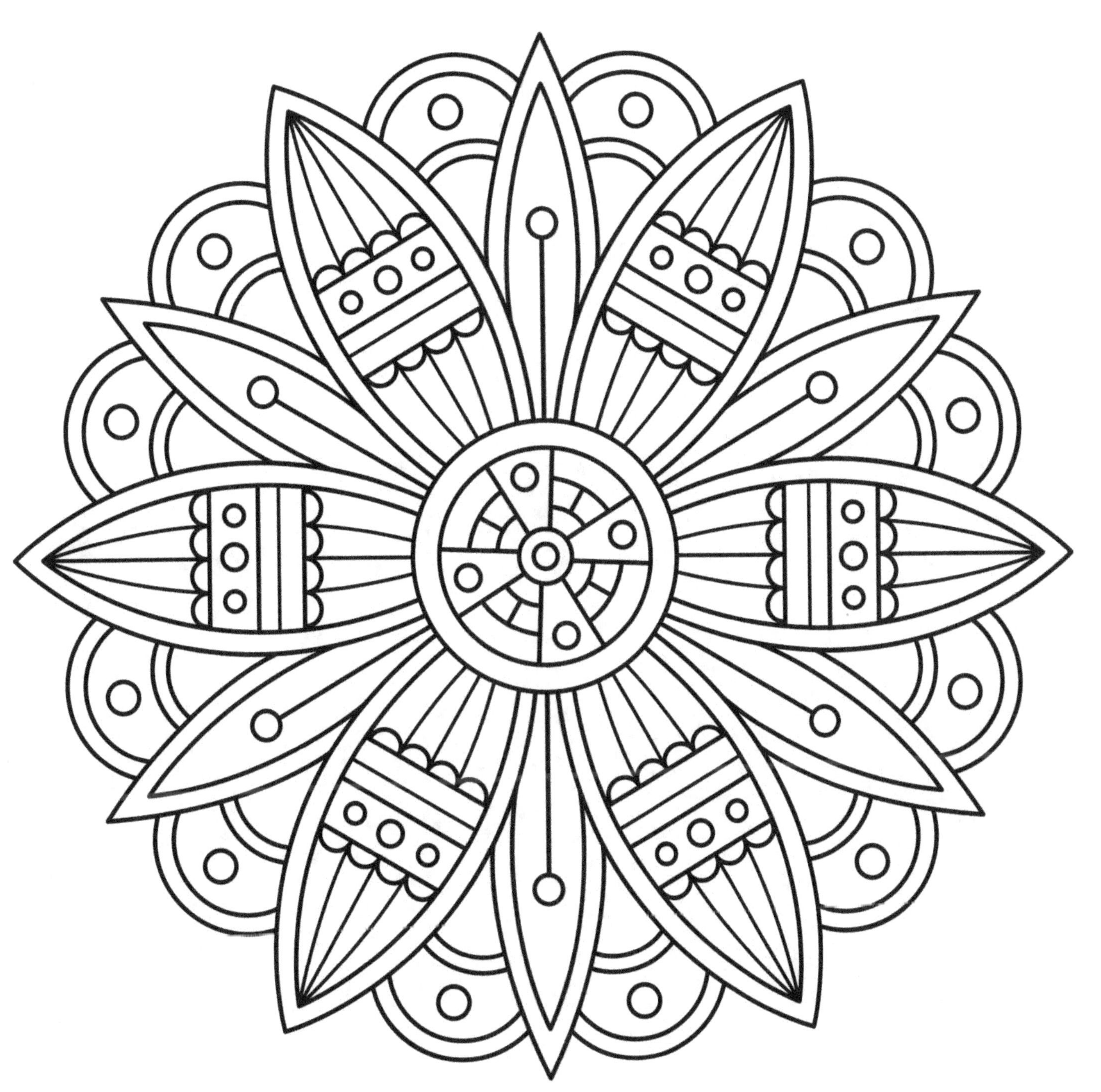

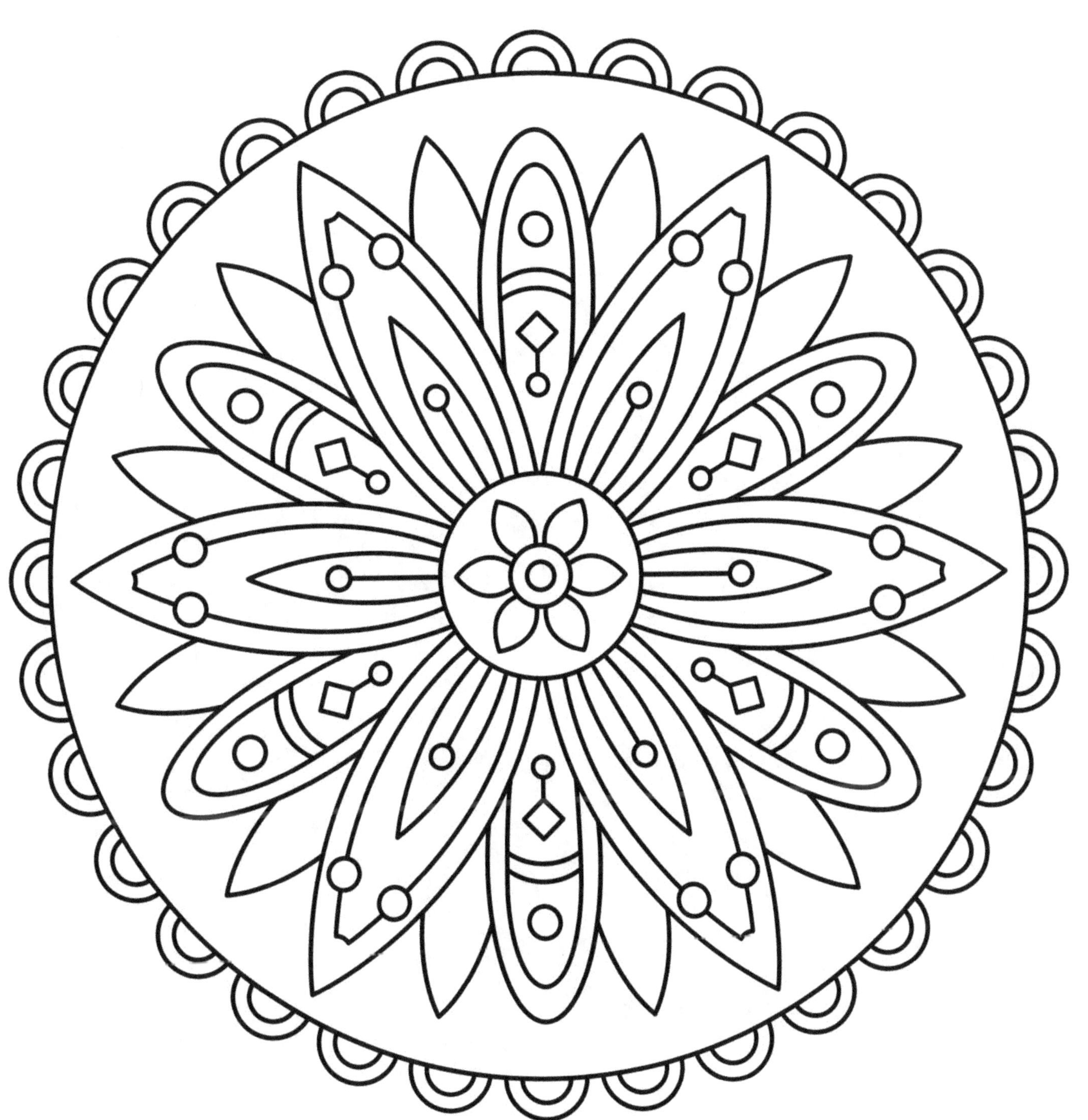

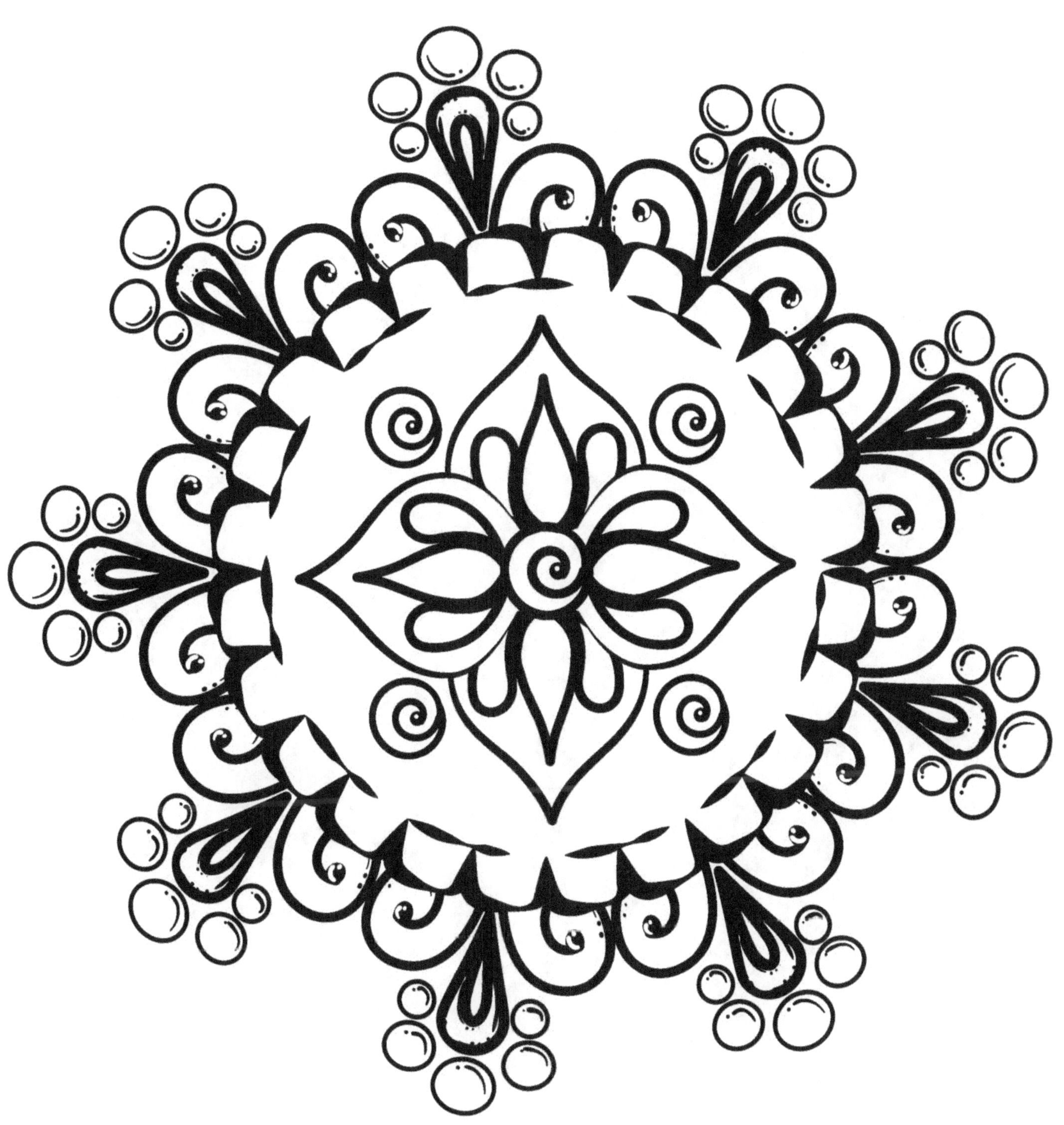

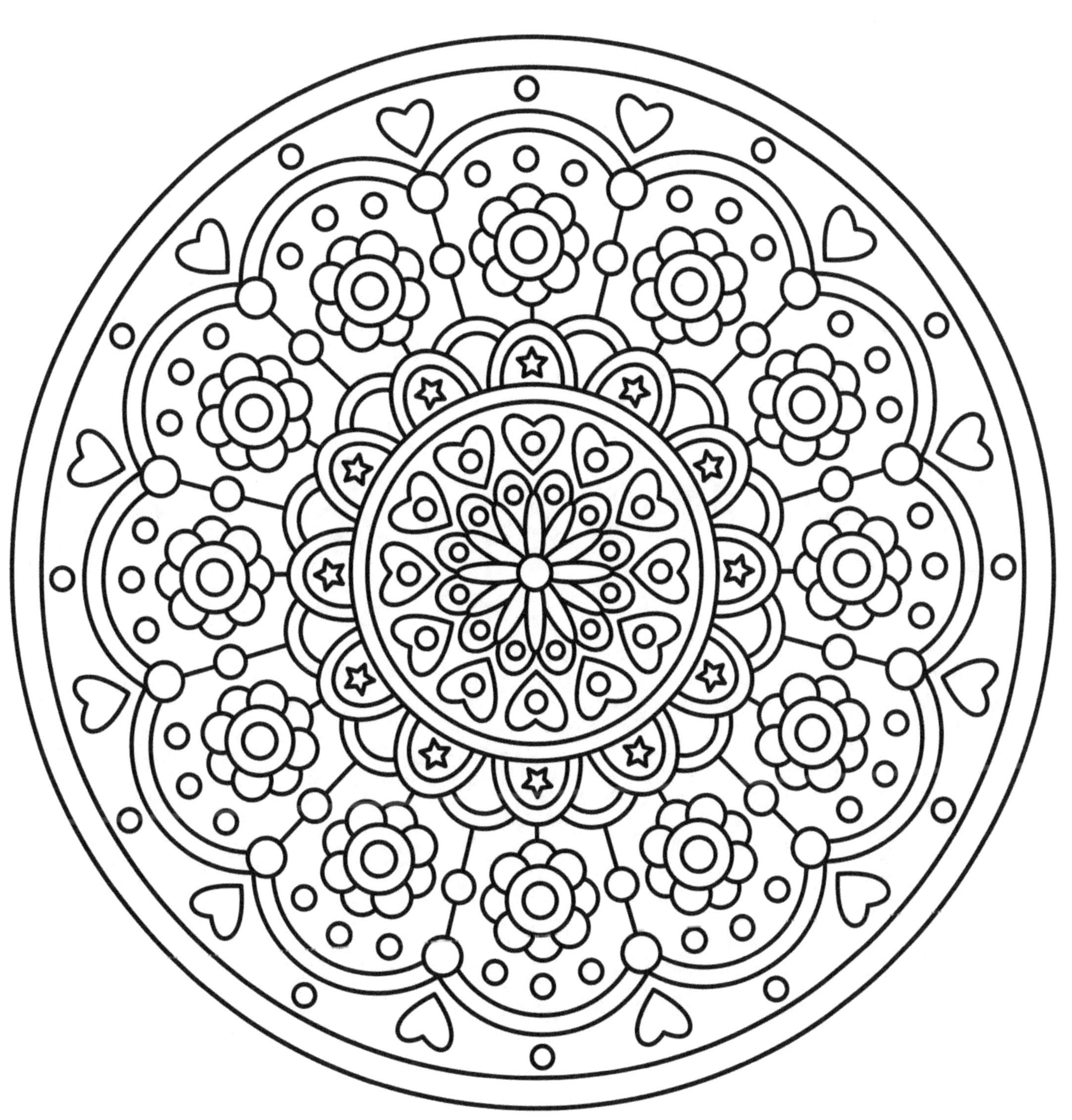

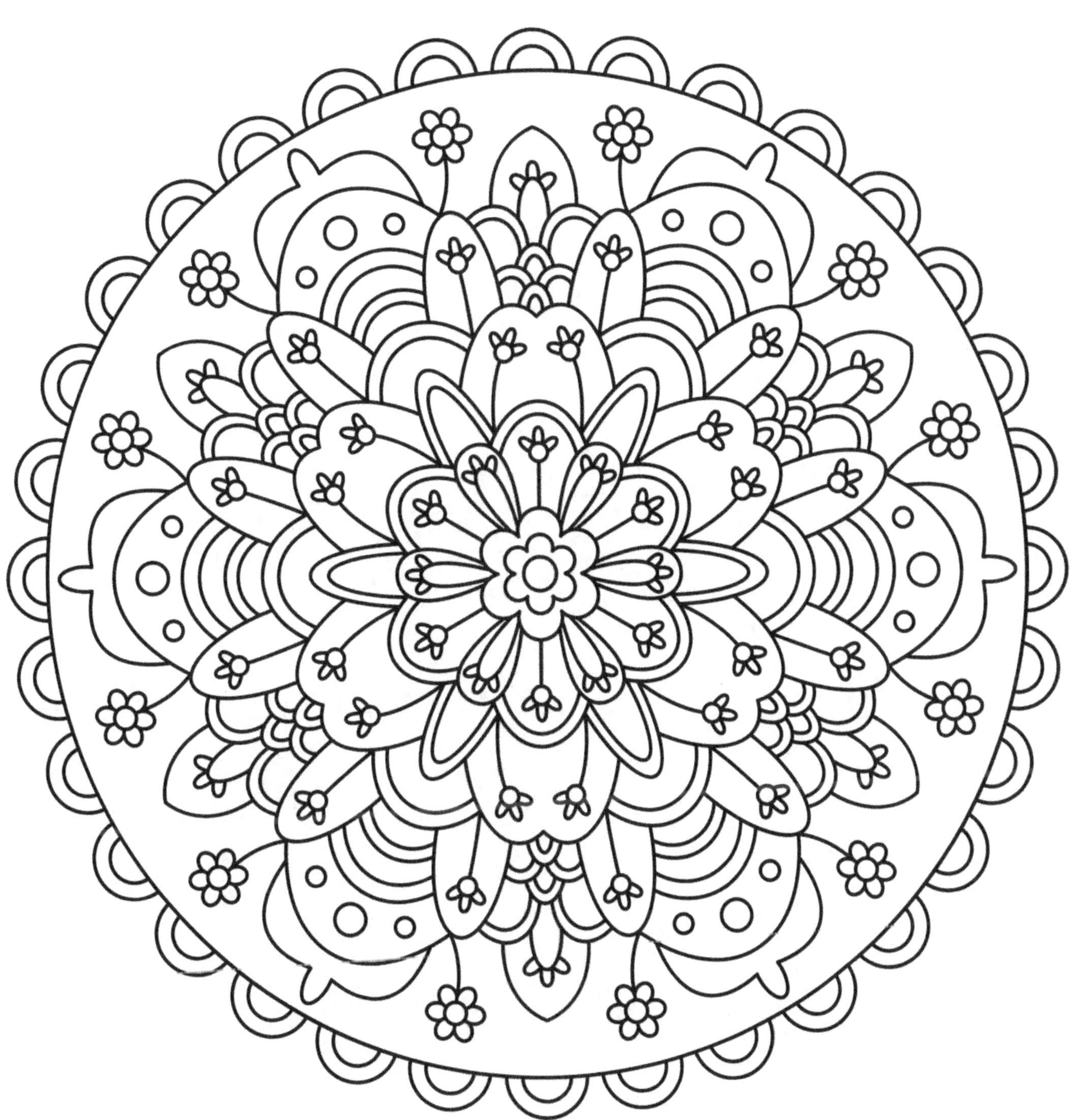

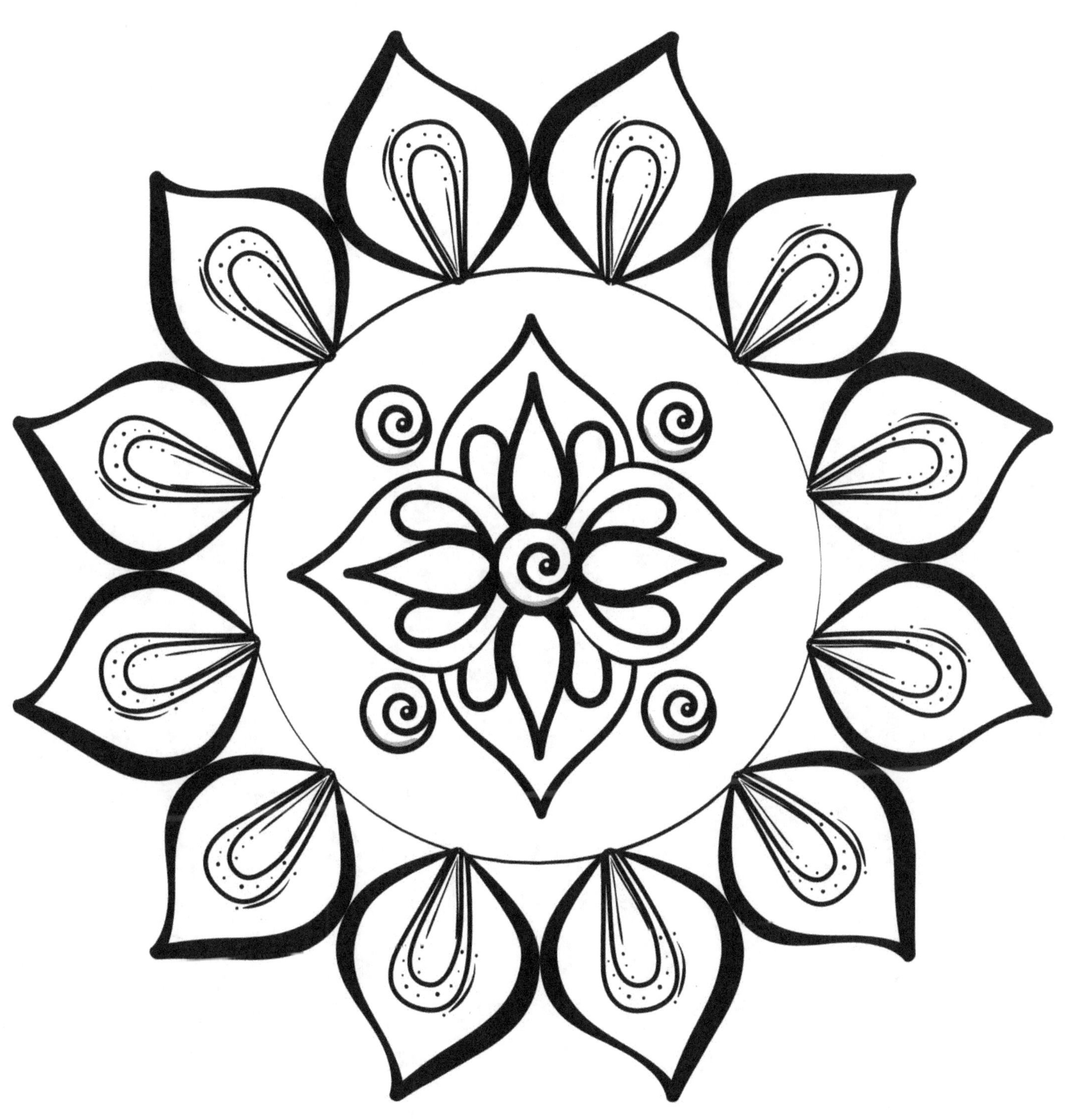

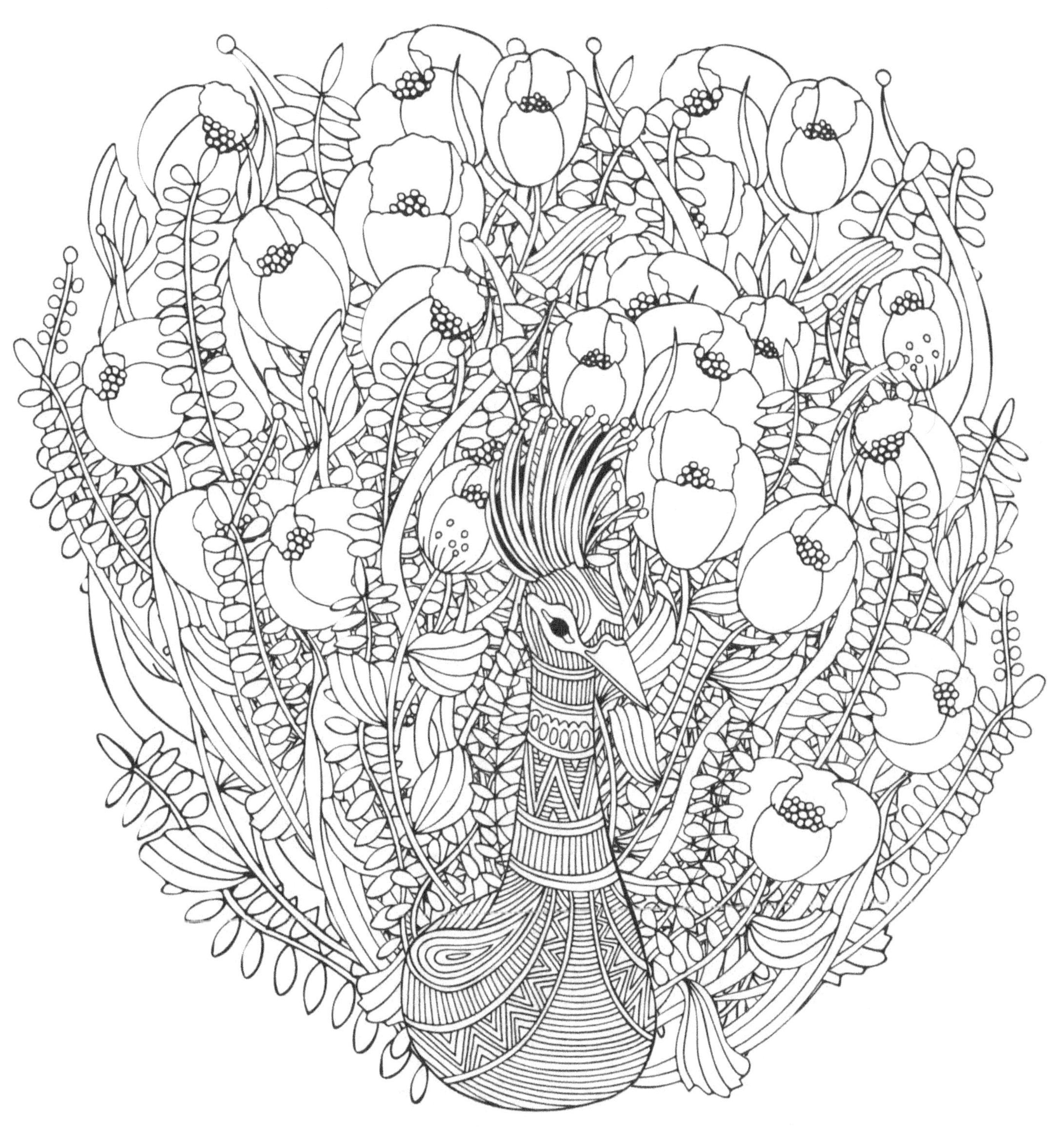